# Letters From Raymond

By Pam Adams

DEDICATIONS:

This book is dedicated to my daughters Janine, Charlene and Hazel, for your constant love and support, for being my very best friends, without whom my life would have been so meaningless. To Duncan and Claire Adams, Ray's son and daughter and my grandchildren: Charné-Carri, Chad, Ryan, Jaden, Kyle and Cody, precious little souls given to us to care for.

May your lives too, be filled with light and unconditional love.

THIS BOOK IS A LOVING TRIBUTE TO:

Ray Adams and Bertie Conradie. Whose love reaches out from beyond the grave!

" You have not gone, you are with us still................"

ISBN 0-620-28064-6

First published 2000

Revised 2009

## Contents

## Introduction

After having lost my husband who was brutally murdered and hijacked in a small town in KwaZulu Natal, I felt that my life had ended. How could I possibly survive losing the most wonderful man that I had ever known? He was my soul mate, my lover and my best friend. But never doubt the powers of the Universe!

I had not lost him at all. In fact I am as close to him now as I ever was. These astounding messages from Raymond from the after life, prove beyond all possible doubt that there is no death. Death is only a beginning. "They that love beyond this world cannot be separated by it".

"When two hearts have joined, the bond becomes a lamp that shines forever".

I hope that by reading my story, your lives too will be changed, that you will be able to find the infinite peace that I have found and that you will have no fear of Death.

The lessons included in this book are the simple universal laws that have been channeled through from Raymond to a well known medium, Beverly Ann Carinus, to whom I owe a debt of gratitude for her patience, time and the inspiration and support that she has given to me.

Hi Stu.

We haven't had a chance to talk properly, so I have resorted to pen to paper. When Reece leaves for wherever, Sally will feel

# *PART ONE*

October 1995, I had been asked to relocate to a busy town in KwaZulu Natal. The company for whom I was working at the time had recently opened their second branch and needed somebody to oversee both branches. I really did not mind, in fact I welcomed the opportunity as I had lived there twice before and still had friends living there with whom I had never lost contact. I had always felt a strange compulsion to go back. A feeling I could not explain even to myself. The memories of the time that I had lived there with my first husband were not happy ones, the heat in summer was unbearable and the crime rate was escalating daily. In fact why did I want to go back? I reasoned with myself. Perhaps I should not, as it was at that stage no longer safe, especially for a woman by herself, but there it was again, that tremendous urgency!

I simply had to move back. Accommodation at that stage was difficult to find, especially for a single woman. After many phone calls I made yet another visit to an estate agent. A very friendly lady took my call and after I had told her about my plight she informed me that she in fact owned a guesthouse and had a room available. That was how I met Joy. I moved in to her lovely guesthouse. Beautifully furnished rooms, each with its own entrance leading out onto the pool area. We soon became firm friends and I settled into my new environment. We spent many hours together, sometimes having her and her husband Piet to dinner. In fact once we got talking we never stopped, so I would cook up a meal on my little stove while they chatted.

I really was happy to be back and enjoyed looking up my old friends. I started doing aqua aerobics in the pool to shape up and persuaded Joy and a few of her friends to join me. We used to meet at the pool at five in the morning. It wasn't long before the inches fell off and we were proudly showing off our nicely toned and tanned bodies. Life settled into a quiet routine once again. I enjoyed my position of being an area manageress for a group of furniture stores. I had enjoyed a highly successful career in sales.

At that stage, having been divorced for nine years, I had decided that I never would remarry. Although I did feel lonely at times I had my family and friends to spend time with. I have never been a party person and although asked out often I did not enjoy ladies nights at pubs. My evenings were spent relaxing in front of the television or reading. I had been staying at Joy's for three months and was quite settled as I had been told that I could sign a year's lease.

Fate has a way of stepping into your life when you least expect it! I was sitting out by the pool one afternoon when Joy walked out with a friend of hers and introduced me to Kate, a lovely vivacious woman who I warmed to immediately. She told me that she was having a party at her house that evening, being New Years Eve 1995 she invited me to come along. I thanked her for the invitation but doubted that I would be able to go. I had my grandson Chad staying with me and could not leave him. We left it at that. Later that evening I had already gone to bed when I heard a knock at the door. It was Kate. "Come along" she said. "No excuses! Chad will be fine with Joy's children." So reluctantly I dressed while she waited. I had mixed feelings. I was basically a shy person and did not enjoy the thought of going to a house party with people whom I did not know.

I walked into the house, the lights were dimmed and most of the furniture had been moved to make room for the dancing. An enormous spread had been laid out on tables around the perimeter of the room. Kate's teenage children and their friends were swinging to loud disco music under a huge ball full of tiny mirrors hanging from the ceiling.

I was handed a drink and introduced to some of Kate's friends. Mainly Civil Engineers, as Kate was a Consulting Engineer herself. I walked over to the table for some snacks and found myself looking into the face of a very distinguished, extremely handsome man who appeared to be in his fifties. He did not look too happy however and seemed uncomfortable at being there. He greeted me and introduced himself. He was wearing an open shirt over bathing trunks. His name he said was Raymond Adams. He mentioned that he was actually meant to be at another party but felt a loyalty to Kate as she had given him so many projects. I could see that he was not enjoying himself.

He seemed to be uncomfortable around crowds. I found it so difficult to speak to him. My mind was reeling. What was it? I knew without any doubt from the second that I saw him that we would be married in a very short time.

He walked away and joined the crowd. I was introduced to a really nice man who I ended up spending most of the evening with. Although we danced and spent time chatting I was totally focused on Ray. At one stage he was dancing with a woman and I felt cheated! In my mind she had no right to be in his arms as he was already mine. I had the strangest feeling that we had always been together.

I went out and jumped into the swimming pool, I had to do something to take my mind off these weird thoughts. "What was happening to me?" I heard someone get into the pool behind me and of all people it had to be Ray. We started to chat. He mentioned that he was staying in a commune as he had only arrived in October, and that he was looking for a place of his own. "I arrived at the same time," I said. "I was fortunate to have found a suitable place to live and was very happy with the arrangements".

After that the lady who he had been dancing with also jumped into the pool. We exchanged a few words and I left them to go in and change. By that time almost everybody had assembled outside to see in the New Year. I was standing behind Ray and he turned around to wish me, and kissed me. Was it my imagination? Or did that kiss linger on just a little too long? There was an unbelievable chemistry between us.

Shortly afterwards I said my good-byes and waited outside for the people who were going to drop me at home. I heard a commotion and looked up to see Ray running out, he motioned for me to wait and rushed over to me and said, "I need your phone number as I believe you might be able to help me find accommodation". I fumbled for a pen and managed to find an eyebrow pencil. Ray handed me a paper serviette and I wrote down Joy's number as I was still waiting for my phone to be installed.

I lay in bed that night wondering what it was. I knew that I had known this person before and that somehow we belonged together. I also knew that I would hear from him soon as this was the man that I would marry. There was no doubt in my mind. All I had to do now was wait for it to happen.

New Years day 1995, I woke up with a feeling of anticipation, something momentous was about to happen. I could not get this man out of my mind. I had promised friends that I would visit them but felt reluctant to go. What if I missed his phone call? I left the house and found myself driving in the direction of where Ray lived. He had told me the address the night before. I drove past his house slowly. There it was again, this feeling that I should be with him! That I belonged to him! That we had known each other before! And yet I knew that I had never met him before the New Year's Eve party.

But! I consoled myself. I need not be concerned; I knew that he was going to call me. Sadly when he did I was not there to receive the call. When I arrived home I was greeted with the news that a gentleman had called but had not left his telephone number.

Back to work after the New Years weekend. I had once again promised friends that I would call in after work and stay to dinner. I had been looking forward to the evening but at four o' clock I called them with an apology. I really had no excuse, how could I tell them that I just felt that I had to get home? I drove home still with the feeling that I was being led, there was something happening to me that I could not explain. As I drove into the driveway I was called to the telephone. It was Ray! He asked if he could call on me as he thought I might know of a place for him to stay. I agreed to see him, wondering what this accommodation story was all about. But if that was what it took to spend time with him I really did not mind. He arrived a few minutes later and we talked and talked for hours. There was something about this man that made one feel safe and secure. I was able to tell him things that I had closed off in my mind for years, chapters of my life that had caused so much pain just seemed to fade away.

Nothing mattered anymore. We never got to talk about the accommodation issue! Later that evening he took me out to dinner. Afterwards I noticed that he was driving out of town. I never bothered to ask where we were going as each moment that I spent with this man was so precious that he could have taken me wherever he wanted to. He drove to a lonely beach and we got out of the car and walked hand in hand for what seemed to be miles. It was a beautiful starry night and we watched the stars as we walked. We both removed our shoes and splashed in the waves like two children.

At that stage I never realized that the beach on which we were walking was one of the most dangerous areas to be in as so many attacks had occurred there. Not a safe place to be! But nothing could have marred this beautiful evening. I watched a shooting star as we walked back to the car and sent up a silent prayer. No man had ever touched me like this, there was something about Ray that reached into the depths of my soul. The fact that he was extremely handsome was just an added bonus. At the age of 52, he was the most stunning man that I had ever met. Beautiful grey eyes and what used to be black wavy hair had almost turned grey. He was well built and one could see that he was used to hard work and the outdoors. He was a picture of good health and vitality!

We said goodbye outside my home and he put his arms around me and held me. Neither of us wanted to part but it was already three o' clock in the morning and we both had to be at work within a few hours.

Ray had mentioned that he had recently taken up parachuting and would be away for the weekend. It seemed to be the longest weekend of my life. He phoned me first thing on the Monday morning to say that he was back and would love to see me again. "What about Wednesday?" he said. There was no way that I could wait until then so I invited him to supper that evening. "I was hoping you would say that," he said and arrived at my place within minutes of our conversation. We spent a romantic evening together and he stayed the night. The next afternoon Ray arrived straight after work, put his head around the door and showed me his toothbrush raising his forehead with a question. I nodded and in he walked with his arms full of clothes, which he had hurriedly grabbed from his cupboard.

So began our time together. From the beginning our relationship never felt new. We were so comfortable together, almost as if we had always been a part of one another's lives. He was so considerate, loving and supportive of anything that I did. There were always little messages or notes that he left for me to find, telling me how much he loved me. Two weeks later he took me to dinner at a charming little restaurant overlooking the harbor. As we sat watching the harbor lights dancing in the swell of the water Ray took my hand and told me that he had never been happier than he was at this moment. The candle burned softly as he asked me to marry him. The love that shone from his eyes was all the confirmation that I needed. A bond had been formed between us both that would last forever.

We were married in September 1995 and were blissfully happy. I had left my job and had started a landscaping business. Ray was once again busy with engineering projects. We lived our life to the full, spending as much time together as possible. I had made a few predictions for Ra, which never failed to amaze him.

I had been concerned at first that he would not accept the fact that I had strong psychic powers, but after I had told him about my gift he was as supportive as ever and encouraged me to continue with my work. Often when he came home late I was able to tell him exactly where he had been before he could even get a chance to tell me. This always resulted in him bursting out laughing as I had accurately described what he had been doing, even to go as far as describing the people that he had just met. I never realized until much later how strong the link was between the two of us.

I had been able to tell him about the communication that I had been receiving from 'The Missing Girls'.  Six little girls, between the ages of 9 and 12 who had been abducted on their way home from school almost 10 years ago. This case was linked to the notorious Gert Van Rooyen and Joey Haarhof.  I had never done automatic writing before and was sitting with a pen and paper one day in 1991 when this strange childish writing started to come through from someone who called herself, 'Lunda'. She begged me to help them contact their mothers.

They started to give me clues and later led me to a monument on the North Coast. I often went to the monument but could not fathom out why I was drawn to it. I used to stand in front of it not really knowing why I was there. I did not know what to do with this information, besides, who would listen to a psychic?  I 'wrote' with them often and felt so helpless, so sad for these little souls who could not rest. I experienced visions of them time and time again. The communication became stronger and the writings increased. Often I would hear from Annamarie or Odette.

I had never told Ray, as I was not sure how he would react to the fact that I was doing automatic writing. I decided eventually to show them to him. He was deeply moved and horrified at the thought that this crime, one of the biggest in the history of South Africa had not yet been solved. "So many children are reported missing, when will it end? Why are we so powerless to prevent this from happening?

So obviously the work of pedophiles that prey on innocent victims for their own pleasure and disgusting needs," he said. He was shattered at this information and desperately wanted to help. This wonderful compassionate man, filled with sadness at what he had just read, sat down next to me and held my hand. "I don't know what we are going to do about it," he said. " But I promise I will find a way". "There has got to be somebody out there who will believe in what you are doing and use the information that you have been given".

It was so wonderful to know that I could share these visions and information with someone who really cared and understood. So many fear the unknown and refuse to become involved or are even prepared to speak about it. With the support that I had from Ray I was prepared to do whatever it took to bring this out in the open. I never anticipated just how the promise that he made to me on that day would manifest.

July 18th, 1996. We were full of anticipation as we started the day. Ray had been offered a permanent position and was to be interviewed that afternoon. This was the answer to our prayers. Although he had at that stage been working for a company, he was not happy.

Ray was an extremely honest man and could not abide lies and deceit. He had been feeling very unsettled in his working environment since he had found out that inferior products were being used in a road construction project that he was supervising. He had also discovered that he was expected to make the intersection narrower than legally required to save on costs.

Ray refused to accept this and had paced up and down the house a few days before, looking extremely worried. He told me that he only had two options, one was to speak to the contractor and the other was to report it to the inspectors. There was no way that he was prepared to compromise his reputation or do anything illegal.

"The client had in fact been quoted on more expensive products and that is what had to be used! Besides the safety of motorists was at stake!" he said.

We never discussed the issue again and I felt that whatever had been worrying Ray had been resolved.

After he left for work that morning I dropped my work team off to finish a garden that we were busy with and drove home to finish some paperwork. I heard the car stop outside and Ray walked in. He walked straight up to me and put his arms around me. "I just had to come and tell you how much you mean to me. I still do not know why you chose to marry me? You could have chosen someone in life who could have given you so much more. I just needed to tell you how much I love you and how truly happy I am," he said.

He held me for a few minutes as if he would never let me go. I assured him that I was quite content and extremely happy. "No amount of money or material possessions could ever replace what we shared. We have everything we need in life, so what are you concerned about?" I asked him. As he started to reverse down the driveway I ran after him, put my arms around him through the driver's window and said, "Know what? I would live in a tent with you. All we need is to be together, nothing else matters". He drove off smiling, really happy, what more could he ask for in life? Perhaps the interview that afternoon would be positive. All he needed to make him really secure was the permanent position that he had been offered. He drove off to the site at one of the rural areas where he was supervising a project a few kilometers outside of town. I had been so concerned when I heard that he would be working there and told him how apprehensive I felt. Ray assured me that he had completed numerous Engineering Projects in that area and was not at all concerned about his safety.

Shortly after he left I drove to the Post Office to collect a parcel that had arrived. His brother Don who lives in America had been a surprise guest at our wedding and had not seen Ray for 13 years, arrived with their brother Norman who had secretly arranged this reunion. Ray was speechless when they arrived that morning. Don took dozens of photographs and promised to send them to us. They had finally arrived and I could not wait to see them.

My youngest daughter Hazel and Ray's son, Duncan, were both staying with us at the time. Duncan had worked late and was still asleep when I arrived home. I called Hazel into my room so that we could look at the photographs and spread them out over the bed. The phone next to the bed rang. It was Ray's employer Heinrich! He asked me if the police had contacted me yet. I said that I had not heard from them. "Why would they want to contact me?" He told me very calmly that Ray had been shot.

The shock of the news rendered me speechless. He told me not to worry, that Ray was fine, that he had been carried by his workers to the clinic nearby and was now being transferred to hospital. He told me that he would meet me there. I had no vehicle at the time as my driver had just left with it. I was in total shock. Hazel woke Duncan and gave him the terrible news. He dressed quickly while Hazel tried to contact my son in law Bruce, who was at that time in a nearby town calling on clients. We needed to get to the hospital and he agreed to fetch us. While we waited outside for him to arrive I tried to convince myself that Ray would be all right. Surely you do not always die from a bullet wound?

On the way to the hospital I insisted that Bruce contact Heinrich on his mobile phone to find out how Ray was. I noticed by the stilted conversation that something was not right. What was he saying? Why would they not tell me? I demanded to know but Bruce said that he had been told not to say anything to me, just to get me to the hospital! A cold chill ran through my body. I want to know now! "Tell me what is wrong!" I almost screamed at him. He spoke quietly, obviously in shock at what he had just heard, "Mom, Ray did not make it. He's gone!" I could hear Duncan gasp with shock while I started to cry hysterically. NO! This can't be true! This could not happen to someone that I loved so dearly!

No! No, Oh please God, tell me that he is alive. It's just one bullet! Lots of people are shot and they survive! Not Ray! Please! Not Ray! We have only been married for 10 months! This is not going to happen! It just cannot be true! Duncan and I sobbed while Hazel tearfully tried to console us. Bruce drove quietly to the hospital and got out to see where Heinrich and his colleagues were. He found them in the outpatients department where they were waiting for me.

The reason that I was to go there, he was told, was so that they could sedate me. I had to find a lift! Drive 20 kilometers! Just to be told that my husband had been murdered! The days of kindly policeman accompanied by a Doctor or a Minister to break ghastly news like this, it seemed, were no more!

I was ushered into the out patients clinic. After almost an hour, the Doctor had still not arrived. The Sister in charge called him once more and was told that perhaps it was best not to sedate me, as I needed to grieve! I should go to his surgery to consult him, approximately 20 kilometers away! I did not want to see anyone! All I wanted was to get home! I could not believe that Ray was dead, there had to be some mistake. He would be waiting for me at home. I got up and walked towards the car. Heinrich followed me and told me how sorry he was and asked me whether I would like to accompany him to the clinic as he was on his way there to identify the body. No! That I could not do! I have always believed that it is better to remember someone in life rather than when they are dead! I could not bear to see him.

I wanted to remember that beautiful smile when he had left me just a few hours ago. Oh my God! How could they have done this to him? This beautiful man, who was kindness itself, had so much to give!! He had finally found the happiness that he deserved. We were so happy and totally in love. Our life together had only just begun, how could he leave me now? We had been looking at properties to build our own home. What about all our plans? What about the promise of this beautiful life that we were to share together?

The police finally arrived at 8.30 that evening. Ray had been murdered at 12 o'clock that afternoon by four black men who shot him three times and hijacked his vehicle. He had walked back to his vehicle to collect his tape measure with a member of his work team.

The hijackers had already 'hot wired' the vehicle and were waiting for him. Why did they not just drive it away? Why did they wait to shoot him? What chance did he have against four men? I was told that at first Ray had tried to argue with them, he had also tried to grab the car keys but must have realized the seriousness of the situation as he turned around and started to run. They shot him in his back!! Why?

I was beginning to have visions about his death. This was no ordinary hijacking! Scenes of the murder were being shown to me! I could not deal with this! Not now! Oh please God! I can't bear it! I cannot possibly allow myself to watch Ray being gunned down! Part of me wanted to know, but I simply did not have the strength to experience a vision of his actual death.

The organ played softly as family, colleagues and friends waited outside of the church. I took my place in the front pew as the pallbearers carried in his coffin and placed it reverently in front of me.

I looked at it and wanted to rip it open! How could Ray be in there? He was so full of life and so real to me still. There was no way I could survive without this man! He was my life and my soul. How would I survive without those constant hugs? Those re-assurances of his total love and devotion!

The service began as we stood up to sing a hymn. I had written a letter to be read in Ray's memory. Brian Lister who conducted the service gently opened the letter and began to read:

"There was never any need to have said goodbye as each day was filled with so much love and tenderness. I could go to sleep at night feeling so fulfilled, happy in the knowledge that everything that needed to be done, had been done, everything that needed to be said, had been said. Our life together was so complete and the love that we shared was so deep, there were no words that could possibly describe it. I was so privileged to have had the time with Ray and so honoured to have been his wife."

I was weeping bitterly at that time and really did not spare a thought of what anybody may have thought. The grief and pain that I felt at his loss was too much to bear. We stood up and sang Psalm 23. As we sang the last verse I looked up! There was Ray! Standing not more than four feet in front of me! As clear as if he were still alive, dressed in his tuxedo, which I had insisted that he would be buried in.

He was standing in front of a huge Fan Palm. There were no plants in the church, so this was part of the vision that I was experiencing. He looked at me for a few moments and smiled, then lifted one of the palm leaves with his elbow while he waved at me with the other hand, crouched a little to go under the leaf and disappeared!

Janine, my eldest daughter, had told me on the morning of the funeral that she kept 'seeing' Ray. There was something that he was trying to tell her. The first vision that she experienced was of him lying face down on the ground, he then lifted himself up she told me, and looked around, he seemed to be terribly confused. After that he appeared to her three more times, pointing to a black leather bag, which had a zip all around. He was desperately trying to get something through to her. He pointed to a side pocket of the bag. What was he trying to tell her? His briefcase had been stolen with the car, and besides it was not round! Also, it never had a zip!

I searched though his cupboard and discovered his black leather hold all. This had a zip that went all the way around the bag. It was empty! I found a pocket on the side, as he had shown her, and opened it. There was a new pocket size packet of Kleenex tissues. I could hardly believe this. Ray had always kept me supplied with those little packets of tissues. He used to keep a packet in the cubbyhole of the cars or in the drawer of his desk.

Since the terrible news I had gone through piles of his handkerchiefs to mop up the tears. He knew that I would need those tissues at the funeral and would not rest until I had found them!

After everybody had left I showered and crawled into my bed. I was emotionally drained! All I wanted was to be by myself. I cried until I fell asleep from sheer exhaustion. Not even sleep could release me from that terrible emotional pain. I woke up soon after and sat up on the bed trying to imagine what I would do without him. I looked up! There he was again! Standing right next to the bed, this time wearing his favorite denims, a sports shirt and his beloved Veldskoens! Ray was frowning and looked terribly worried. He had his hand stretched out to me and on it was a crumpled piece of paper. I was only to find out the day after what that crumpled piece of paper meant.

The insurance consultant arrived and I ushered him into Ray's study. He offered his condolences and expressed his shock and concern at the terrible tragedy. Justin looked really uncomfortable! I could see that he found it difficult to be with me. It was only two months prior to that day that he had consulted Ray and I, to draw up a joint will. He took a deep breath, cleared his throat and fidgeted in his chair, "Pam, there is something that I have got to tell you". I looked at him. What was wrong? Why was this man so uncomfortable?

He hesitated for a while and finally plucked up the courage to speak, "I have been slack". He paused for a while and then finally gave me the news that he had come to tell me. "I forgot to process the will. I am so sorry". That means of course that the previous will that Ray had made years ago in favor of his ex-wife was still valid.

I was so numb from shock at that stage that I really did not care. I could not possibly discuss this issue. Nothing mattered to me. I just wanted my husband back. I could not accept that he was not coming home anymore. I was still in my shock and grief, making two cups of coffee instead of one, still switching on the kettle at five fifteen in the afternoon to have his coffee ready as he walked through the door.

Still! Without thinking! Dishing up two plates of dinner instead of one! What was he talking about? This was only a bad dream that I was having! How could it be true? There was no future without Ray! I did not care how I would survive!

I had to get back to work, clients were waiting and my work team seemed lost. They had no direction anymore! They used to enjoy all the fun in the mornings as Ray chivvied them along to load the equipment on to the trucks, joking and bantering with them. He never left until he knew that my vehicles were loaded and that they were filled with fuel and the oil and tires had been checked.

He used to rush off to the shop and buy cold meats and loaves of bread for each worker, making sure that they were looked after. Nothing was too much for him.

They had taken the news so badly. My thoughts flew back to the day of the funeral. As I walked out of the church, I noticed that they had all congregated outside to pay their respects. There they stood, seventeen men dressed in their best clothes, holding their hats in front of them as a sign of respect. I walked over to thank them. Old 'Mr. Dube' as I fondly called him, had tears streaming down his face, as did many of the others. They greeted me sadly and motioned that they wished to speak to me. Mr. Dube began his little speech, "Mama, our Baba has gone. Taken away by those' Totsies'! But! You must never worry Mama, because all of us, we are here to look after you. You are our Mama, so we must look after you," he said.*

The respect of these black people touched me so deeply as they all, one by one, came and shook my hand. How could I not go on? I had a commitment to these people who were prepared to protect me and work with me. They gave me the strength to go on, without their help I would have just given up.

'Mr. Dube' passed over soon after Ray! I still think of his kindness and support, his sense of humor and willingness to work, even though he was suffering from cancer he simply refused to stay at home. "I am here for you Mama," was all he would say when I insisted that he go home. He would just shake his head, "I must look after you". I frantically sent him to doctors but sadly there was nothing that anyone could do for him. He had been such a loyal friend and a constant source of laughter to us all. We all missed him.

Messages were coming through to me once more. I could feel that Ray was around and often felt his presence. There were times when I could feel his arms around me. I felt his fingers running through my hair. The kettle would switch on by itself! This usually happened when I had been contemplating making some tea. One night while I was in the bath I felt water being poured over my back! There was no shower that could be dripping water on to my back and besides! The water was the same temperature as the bath water! I knew what it was.

*The black people often call their employers 'Mother' or 'Father' as a sign as respect. * Totsie! A Zulu name for scoundrel.

There was no doubt that Ray was around again. I knew that he was deeply concerned about me. I had received a phone call from Heinrich informing me that I need not worry. As he said he would see that I would be looked after financially.

Ray had been a permanent member of his staff he said, which meant he would have been covered by Workman's Compensation. He also told me of an insurance policy that had been taken out on Ray's life by his company! "That was something that he did for all his employees," he said. I would receive some of that money he assured me.

A few days later I received another phone call from him, apologizing because there would be no financial help after all. "It would not be possible," he said, to pay me any money from the insurance. Also, he regretted that there would be no Workman's Compensation either! "Because Ray was a contractor and not a permanent staff member!" he said. I knew then that there was something terribly wrong! There was no doubt that Ray had been employed on a permanent basis. He had come home one evening and given me the news. We discussed the fact that the salary was lower than he would have expected but as he now had a permanent position at least he felt more secure. He did not trust Heinrich for some reason and had told me so on numerous occasions.

The shock of what he had just told me threw me back into depression. How would I cope? At the age of 50 it was not easy to find employment. What was I going to do?

I have always been positive, my faith and my belief have never let me down. I would survive, no matter what.

But! Where would I start? Once again I felt that Ray was trying to tell me something. What was it? It was difficult to concentrate, feeling as low as I did. Finally the message got through, "Phone the compensation office". Now why would I do that? I had already being informed that there was no point! The 'urging' got stronger! I could feel his frustration. Okay! If that's what you want, then I will do it!

So began the long process of trying to convince them that Ray had been permanently employed. As to their knowledge, and according to the information given to them by Heinrich, Ray was only a Contractor, which meant that I would not qualify! Although I had no written proof of the discussion between the two of them of being permanently employed I was told that a verbal agreement was binding and advised to proceed with the application.

The communication from Ray was coming through more frequently! He wanted me to move down to the South Coast to build a Retreat. This was for the purpose of helping people who had suffered a loss and for those who had lost direction in their lives. Now how would I possibly do that? I wondered! How would I ever be able to afford to do this? I can't even support myself let alone build a retreat! "What I needed for this project would be provided," I could hear him telling me.

I believed one could communicate and knew I had strong psychic powers and yet I had never experienced any messages as strong as those I received from Ray. So few of us believe it is possible. I was now convinced that these visions given to me were from him.

He was communicating through me 'By thought'! I heard little things that he always used to say. It was amazing! I tripped over a rug and heard him say just like he used to, "Ya silly thing! Now look what ya gone and done!" I could hear him chuckle! Ray was around! I could never forget his warm and infectious laugh.

Members of the South African Police approached me two months after Ray's passing. They had been shown some of the writings from the 'girls' by a reporter who had leaked them to the police.

Tremendous pressure was being put on me to help with the case. At that stage, only a few weeks after my own loss, I did not want to get involved. After a few days and many requests from a member of the occult crime division, I agreed to meet them with the forensic team at the Monument, which had been shown to me by the girls.

The Monument had been erected in the year 1902 by the parents of a young man who had been washed off the rocks. This is where I first sensed the presence of the girls. I had been there a few years ago and taken photographs of a friend sitting on the wall of the tidal pool. My friend had lost her mother. I was astounded when I had the photographs developed! There in the background of one of these prints were three people! The picture of the woman, who I recognized immediately, was the mother of my friend. A young man wearing very old fashioned bathing trunks, stood with his hands on his hips and one foot resting on the wall of the tidal pool. I could see the water glistening on his body as if he had been swimming. In the middle of the print, was the face of a beautiful little girl! These were spirits that had been captured on film!! I compared the face of the girl to the photographs of the missing girls and knew that it was 'Annemarie Wapenaar'. Shortly after, I began to receive the automatic writing. I was in no doubt this was a link with the missing girls.

Whilst I was standing at the monument with the crime unit and the forensic team I experienced a vivid vision of the girls. Never before had I experienced anything like this! I was shown a derelict house and was able to describe it for them accurately. I was also able to tell them what Annemarie Wapenaar was wearing when she was abducted. This was proved later to be an exact description of her outfit. I had told them that it was new, giving them the colour and description of the outfit and also that it was the first time she had ever worn it.

I was later shown the house by the police, close by the monument, which fitted the exact description of the one I had seen in the vision.

Many of the writings mentioned the name 'Johan'. I felt this person was the young man who had been washed off the rocks and had linked up with the two missing girls who had passed over in the same area. The inscription on the monument read:

> *In loving memory of Albert H. J. Frerikson. Born Dec 24th 1886. Washed off the rocks and drowned July 19th 1904, aged 17 years. This stone was erected by his parents, looking for the resurrection of the body when the sea shall give up her dead.*

The crime unit later established and confirmed that his parents had called the young man 'Johan'! I could sense the 'girls' around me, excited at the prospect of finally being found. After many investigations by the occult crime unit I lost contact with the people with whom I had been dealing. Different members of the crime unit approached me again, almost two years later. Investigations were carried out! Police dogs were brought in, which reacted positively to areas that were shown to them.

New evidence came to light and was sent to the forensic laboratory. Once again we waited in anticipation but nothing happened. Ray was beginning to send information through regarding the girls. I often saw them together in visions. There was no doubt in my mind the promise Ray made in life was now being carried out from the afterlife. It was as if he made it his mission to solve the mystery of those little girls.

Sadly, to this day the case remains unsolved. More information was channeled through and passed on to the inspector handling the case. This time in a different area where I was told, “Many bodies will be found!”

# *Part Two*
# *LETTERS*

I asked my nephew to take over the business, as at that stage I had built up so many good contracts and did not want to see my staff without employment. I said my good-byes to those loyal people who worked so hard for me. Once again they all congregated to see me off and cried for their "Mama" who was leaving them. I was so numb with pain that emotionally I felt I could not take anymore. I had not slept well for months and desperately needed to rest. Although I secured a house at the Kwa Zulu South Coast and had no idea what lay ahead of me, I had no doubt that I would be led. I could feel that my life had changed dramatically. I was on a totally different path and was prepared to accept that without question.

Ray appeared to me often. At first I would see him in his earthly clothing, clothes that I remember so well. I felt a little nervous at first. This was awesome! The visions of him were so clear, almost as if he had never gone away. I reasoned with myself that if I never feared him in life then why would I fear him in death?

I relaxed and welcomed any possibility of seeing him again. The messages were more frequent and I felt safe knowing he was still taking care of me. I could feel this incredible love that surrounded me. I was disturbed one night by dogs barking. I lived alone in a huge house, the only one I had been able to find at the time and was very nervous.

I lifted myself up and leaning on my elbow, reached out to pull the curtain aside to see what the disturbance was all about. There seemed nothing worth concerning about so I closed the curtain and looked down at my pillows to straighten them before I settled down again. Ray was there, right next to me, his head on the pillow! I felt incredibly happy and just lay down to go back to sleep, secure in the knowledge that he was there. A few weeks later I was awake and it was fairly late. I was sitting on the bed with my back against the headboard reading. I felt his presence and looked up. He was sitting on the bed with his hand on my knee. He looked wonderful, wearing a form fitting light blue shirt that had silver specks woven into the fiber of the fabric. His hair seemed longer than usual, but beautifully combed and neat. He smiled at me and sat there for a few minutes. I saw him again a few days later wearing a beautiful blue robe. The fabric I noticed was of high quality, soft pleats that fell loosely off the shoulders and a 'priests' collar made in the same fabric edged with gold. He stood and watched me for a while, smiled and left.

I was sitting at my electric typewriter one day, trying to complete a reading for one of my clients, when Mittens, my beautiful black Persian that had grieved terribly for Ray after his passing, disturbed me. She had brought something for me from outside which she was proudly trying to show me. I thought that it might be a gecko and chased her away. All of a sudden the typewriter jammed! I could not understand it! There had been nothing wrong a few minutes ago so why would it not work? I called my daughters in but none of us could find any reason why it should have jammed. I could not continue and decided to take it in the next day to be repaired. My maid discovered while cleaning the following day, a huge poisonous spider under the table that the typewriter was on. I switched the typewriter on and it worked beautifully. I knew once again that it had to have been Ray who was protecting me. Little incidents kept happening around the house, more confirmation that I was being looked after.

Whilst driving to Durban one morning I felt a little nervous, as some motorists had recently had bricks thrown at their windscreens! One of them had been fatally injured. I noticed a bright light on the seat next to me and looked across to see that Ray was beside me, protecting me as usual. I could feel his hand on my leg as if to reassure me that I was safe.

My two daughters Hazel and Charlene decided to relocate and moved in with me. The house was once again filled with laughter and activity. I began to feel alive. It was wonderful to spend time with my grandchildren, who unknowingly pulled me back to life again.

I had never forgotten my purpose for moving to the South Coast, I knew without any doubt that I would build this retreat and waited for a sign that would tell me to proceed. When I mentioned this project to my family and children, I could see that they doubted me. However, they placated me by agreeing that it would be a wonderful idea. I could see by the knowing looks that they gave one another that they did not believe I could do it.

I received a letter from a woman who I had briefly met just before I left to relocate to the South Coast. Yvonne had contacted me to restore her garden and I arranged to meet her at her home. I met her outside her gate and introduced myself. At first I felt really uncomfortable! she seemed so unresponsive and difficult to communicate with. She showed me around and we discussed the fee. I promised to start right away. As I was leaving she mentioned that it had been her husband who had been shot a few months previously and asked whether I knew about it.

Bert Conradie was the Sheriff and had been brutally gunned down by a client of ours when he went to attach some vehicles. I recall the episode with horror.

I had been in the area when it occurred. Janine and I had teamed up and we should have been at one of her clients Louis Nel, to do his garden service. For some reason, perhaps fate had a hand in it, we decided against going to his house on that particular day. We heard on the car radio whilst driving home that there had been a terrible shooting. The Sheriff, his Deputy Les Moore, and a man from one of the Transport Companies had been gunned down and were fatally wounded.

They had been shot with shotguns. I can remember arriving home at the time and Ray asking me whether I had heard the news. We were so saddened at the brutality of the murders. (How could we have known that within two months Ray was to suffer the very same fate?). Louis Nel, financially destitute and depressed about the liquidation of his company, had snapped. He later took his own life in prison.

I could understand now why Yvonne seemed so bitter and offered her my condolences. I told her who I was and she recalled Ray's shooting. How strange that fate should throw us together after we had both lost our beloved husbands. I desperately wanted to help Yvonne but did not know how to approach her. I mentioned that I was psychic and that perhaps I could help. Yvonne gave me a strange look and brushed me off. I left it at that. Whilst speaking to her on the phone a few days later, I laughed when she explained that she thought that I was a ventriloquist! She wondered how I could possibly help her 'by throwing my voice'! Being Afrikaans, that is how she had interpreted what I had told her.

I explained that I could give her Spiritual help. Unfortunately, as much as she wanted me to visit and help both her daughters and herself there was no time, I was already packing and about to leave within a few days.

Yvonne's letter was filled with sadness. She was struggling to cope with the loss of her husband. They were married for 20 years. Bert, who was 48 years old, had left behind a broken hearted wife and two teenage daughters! She simply could not accept his death and asked for help. Was there anything that I could do?

I replied to her letter and whilst I was writing I could feel Bert around me. He began to communicate with me. I was able to tell her how they met, how he had struggled to convince her to marry him. Things that I could not possibly have known! Yvonne called me soon after receiving my letter. She was in total awe of what she had just read. She could not believe what I had told her.

Yes! That is how it happened! I was able to give her more information on the phone and asked her who 'Boekie' was? That was his pet name for his youngest daughter, she explained. The next question that I asked left her speechless, "Yvonne, what has happened to the red vehicle which you sold after Bert's death, the one that was never licensed? What did you say?" She asked. I repeated the question and waited while Yvonne tried to compose herself. "But how could you know that"? She said "I only sold that vehicle long after Bert had passed away!! Nobody knows about it other than me and my daughter!" I explained that the information that I had received from him was perhaps because he was worried about it and also wanted her to believe that he was in fact still around. I later helped Yvonne to trace the person who had purchased the vehicle as she had lost touch with her. It was then resold and licensed.

Yvonne phoned every evening at 7 0' clock without fail. That was our 'prime time' she said. She started to accept and to heal. She had been made Acting Sheriff when Bert passed on and was waiting for her official appointment. She asked me one day why I had moved down to the South Coast? I told her about the message from Ray, that he wanted me to build a retreat. "Lets do it!" she said. "Go out and find the land tomorrow". That was the beginning of our partnership.' Raybert Lodge', was going to happen after all. I set out early the next morning to find a suitable property.

Eventually I found what I believed to be the right property, further down the Coast. But! It was not to be. I was woken up in the middle of the night with a feeling that I must look at the property section in our local paper. Not Now! I pleaded, but the feeling would not go away. I opened the property section and immediately spotted a small advertisement - "Owner needs to sell urgently". I called early the next morning and arranged an appointment to view.

I had found the right spot inland from the beach, with magnificent sea views, huge indigenous trees, enormous Flat Crowns, Beautiful Milk wood trees, Avocado and Mango trees. There was a spiritual energy that made one feel so peaceful, a tranquility that I had not felt in a long while. I knew that the message I had received the night before had led me to this place. It was simply meant to be.

Before I had time to wonder what we would build. I was shown this incredible vision. Of course Log Cabins! Little cabins situated amongst those beautiful trees. It was all there! We never had to plan it as it had already been decided. We were later able to purchase the two adjoining properties. Although I had been told that the person who owned them would never sell, "Not in a million years," I was told. "He has plans passed and has started to develop a low cost housing scheme." I was not about to be put off and contacted the developer. "Absolutely not!" he said. "Can't you see that I have started building?" I could see that he was intrigued with my determination and he asked why I wanted to purchase the property. I drove over to his site and explained about our spiritual quest and could not believe my luck when he agreed to sell.

I had heard from Heinrich again. Out of the blue he called to say that I should contact the commissioner's office and get them to fax him a form as soon as possible. "I am prepared to sign now," he told me. Ray did work for me! "So you see there is a light at the end of the tunnel!" he said. I could hardly believe this! What had made him have a change of heart?

I immediately gave the commissioners office the news. They contacted him within minutes of me phoning them but once again he refused! I called him to ask what was going on. "I have changed my mind," he said quietly and refused to discuss it any further. What was this man playing at? I instructed my attorney to proceed with an appeal. Two and a half years after Ray had died I finally won the case. It was proved that Ray had been employed. Although Heinrich had been issued a subpoena to appear at the actual commissioners hearing, he did not turn up. The case was granted in my favour. I was to receive a lump sum for the time that had lapsed and a pension for the rest of my life. I could now put this issue to rest and concentrate on the building project.

I was in constant touch with the Murder and Robbery unit regarding Ray's murder. Nothing seemed to be forthcoming. I could not believe that no arrests had been made! Ray's petrol card had been used two days after his death at a local service station. His vehicle had been used in a robbery in the same area a few days later. I had given them so much information that had been described to me in visions. Actual descriptions of the people who I believed were responsible for Ray's murder - their age, descriptions of their features and their build!

At one stage I was informed that I had just described a person who was already in custody and that further investigations regarding this person would be made. The case has been transferred from one person to another, from one area to another. I had written to the chief of police who subsequently arranged for the area commissioner to call on me. I was assured that everything possible was being done. To this date, more than five years have passed and his murder remains unsolved. Ray's death has become another statistic in the ever-escalating list of crimes in South Africa.

I made an appointment to call on Bev, a psychic, for a consultation. Although I had moved on with my life, I was severely depressed. I wondered if the pain, that terrible void that I felt, could ever heal. Bev did a reading for me and accurately predicted that I had suffered a loss. I told her that I had lost my husband but never gave her Ray's name or told her how he had died.

A few weeks later I received a letter from Bev in the post. I had written to her asking for a reading for Yvonne, and given her my forwarding address. Nothing could have prepared me for the shock I was about to receive when I opened her letter:

*Dear Pam,*

*Many thanks for the letter received. I've been waiting for you to contact me I do not have a phone number or address for you and last week after talking to Yvonne and while in the middle of doing a postal reading, suddenly and quite unexpectedly, got the urge to write, only afterwards did I realize it must be for you. So it was a great relief to get your letter, which had a return address for you. I will rewrite the letter for you, as sometimes, automatic writing can be difficult to read. Firstly, his presence was very gentle, relaxed and calm. He must have been a very well mannered, polite man, as this came through very strongly. Herewith:*

## Letter One

*Greetings Bev,*

*May I call you that? I come in the name of the Lord and bless you for the work that you do in aiding others, especially Pam.*

*It means so much. I am sorry but I do get so emotional. One has certain feelings in spirit. It's just a shift of consciousness, so please excuse me. I never have been a person of 'if only', but I have to say, if only I had known and held her in my arms and said goodbye, we would both be so much at peace. Please tell her that our love is eternal and will transpire all else. I am with her day and night. I touch her and wipe away the tears and feel so frustrated. I will not leave her, my soul mate. The bond is so great, Universal! I was never a great writer or even able to express my feelings and now they overwhelm me. Forgive me Bev. I'm just concerned for her to know that I love her and that I'm there. I won't take up any more of your time, please give this message to her.*

*Bless you,*

*Raymond*

I was so overwhelmed! This caused a spate of weeping which was desperately needed in order to heal.

I compared the signature on the original automatic writing to one of Ray's documents and found that it was exactly the same. There was no doubt that this was Ray's. This was to be the beginning of regular correspondence from Ray. I could hardly wait for the next one to arrive. I realized that I could not ask for this kind of communication. I was so afraid each time I received one it would be the last. Perhaps this was the manner in which he would say goodbye to me? Never in my wildest dreams did I ever imagine that this was to be the beginning of regular letters coming through from the afterlife.

## Letter Two

*Blessings! May the Lord bless you and keep you in his white light of protection.*

*Hello Beverly,*

*Thank you for your time once again. You know it is so strange, because in my earthly existence I did not believe in any of this, only what I could see and feel, you know, the proven routes. Thank Heavens we have enlightened beings like you and Pamie, to help us with communication and guidance. It has always been very difficult for me to communicate my feelings and more so through another and so I do thank you. Sure I can and do communicate with Pam, but you know, like I said about the strange human element of self- doubt and proof! So herewith: Darling little one, I love you, love, love, love you. Take heart, my life's events are paving out for you. Hope will be restored. I get so mad at the half-truths and cover ups, but everything will come out in the end. To think I called him 'friend', but you dear heart, always did warn me. Time will be advantageous to you, so continue to have courage, knowing that I am at your side constantly.*

*Pamie, believe me, to everything there is a plan and a purpose, even when chaos surrounds one. It's time love to choose words very carefully and be guided by your gut feelings. They won't let you down and I am always around. You have so much inner strength and divine beauty. This time apart was meant to be but by no means can time, distance or universal space, separate us. We are bound by universal energy! And my sweet love, we spend time together. I know you are feeling low, but you will find that you are going to be so busy. Accept Darling, its part of the plan. Love you and I reach out and touch you with the white light of Peace and Protection.*

*I am always there loving you,*

*Raymond.*

Ray had always told me that he loved me, three times! Once was never enough! More confirmation! There was no doubt that these messages had in fact come from him. He had also always shortened my name to 'Pamie'

## LETTER THREE

*Greetings, I come in the White Christ Light, with many blessings for you and much protection and guidance. We thank you for your time.*

*My dearest love,*

*Moments like these are so precious. Even though I am constantly by your side I sometimes feel so frustrated at not being able to reach out to you and physically take you in my arms and ease your pain and burdens. I am near, and your plans are Gods plans and therefore they will manifest and you will see the reasons for the delays. Everything will come right. I am 'progressing' so much on the spiritual path and one day will be able to project my image to you. Already you feel me there but soon you will see me too. The physical manifestation is not important to me, for your very essence is in me and I in you. Yet, you will glance into the mirror and I will be there. It is hard work for me but it will make you happy my love. Together we are going to do much great work -'I from this side and you from your side'. 'Meant to be!' We are never parted. You are helping me with my work here. I love you, love, love and love you, now and in all eternity. Yours, always, with light and eternal love, I surround you, protect you and heal you.*

*Always yours,*

*Raymond*

I desperately needed at this stage, to have some confirmation that there would be some light at the end of the tunnel. We had been experiencing endless problems with the building contractor, but after receiving these messages from Ray I began to feel more optimistic and even more determined to succeed.

## Letter Four

*Dearest One,*

*I have been close to you for I feel your pain and your sense of loss, but love, we are soul mates and therefore there can be no separation, no ending! We are bound by spirit. I am to direct and guide you until we can be together once more. I have been furthering my lessons on this side. There is so much to learn, but as I grow, you do too. There is a band of protection around you at present. This is because you are going into an area where there are people and situations of low spiritual vibration. So you are given spiritual protection so as not to affect the work and vibration level we have together. You are very often entering the astral plane at night, and joining me in the astral; To help with rescue work and helping those that have passed over as suddenly as I did; To see the white light and accept that they too need to move on without trauma or fear. You too receive much healing and energy at this time.*

*You cannot retain the memory for you would want to stay and you have much work to accomplish. The purest of thoughts and vibrations you receive in the astral and our meetings, gives you the strength to continue. Right now, things don't have to work out to a plan in order for you to benefit from them. Everything is working out to a Gods plan. Be patient a little longer, there is much achievement coming your way. There is so much I could tell you about our bond.*

*Forever love always,*

*Raymond*

I had suffered another loss, my beautiful black cat Mittens, had been killed by the dogs next door and I was devastated.

Although, at this stage we had started to build the lodge, I had so many questions in my mind. I wished that I would be given more information. How had this been planned? Please just show me something! Some little indication that I was doing the right thing! A few days later my prayers were answered. I experienced an extraordinary vision. Whenever I am about to experience a vision, I feel a strange power surge through my head.

It would frighten me at first but I had accepted it as part of my spiritual path and was quite used to it by now. I felt the usual humming sound and suddenly found myself in a strange place.

I was standing in a huge building, made of heavy logs. It appeared to be a workshop of some sort, as there was a workbench along the entire area of the surrounding walls. I noticed piles of architects plans rolled up in their folders, propped up against the wall. There was a set of plans opened up and lying on the workbench. Ray stood in front of these plans, holding them down with the palms of his hands. He was wearing a short blue robe with capped sleeves, tied at the waist with a cord.

I stood next to him and looked down at the plans and was astounded to see that they were the plans of Raybert Lodge! This was unbelievable!! They were actually the same plans! How could this be? This was not a dream. I was actually there and I knew that I had been there many times before. That is all that I was shown and realized how truly blessed I was, to have been 'allowed' to experience this vision.

I knew without any doubt that these were in fact God's plans, and yes, they would manifest. I was so intrigued with what Ray had written about the astral and wished that I could remember what I had seen whilst I was there. My wishes were to be granted. A couple of nights later I again experienced a vision. I heard the usual humming sound and found myself to be once again in the astral.

This time I was standing at the exit of what appeared to be a tunnel. An angel with huge wings was positioned on top. As we waited for someone to arrive, an old man appeared, wearing a hospital gown. He had straight white hair, almost bald on top. He appeared to be confused, not knowing where he was. The helpers reached out, took his arms and gently guided him through.

Once again I had been given proof.

There was no death, only a transition – 'The beginning of a journey into the beyond'. That was the 'rescue work' that Ray had written about.

The 'letters' were coming through more frequently now and could hardly wait for the next one to arrive. I began to heal and life took on a new meaning. I could survive anything whilst I still had Ray with me!

Yvonne continued to phone me at her usual time and was enthralled with what I had to tell her. I often felt Bert around and was able to give her little messages, which changed her perspective on life completely.

It was wonderful to be able to communicate with him. I could feel that both Ray and Bert were helping us with the building project. I had never done anything like this before and yet knowledge that I needed was being channeled through to me.

At one stage I had begun to feel very uneasy and could sense that there was something happening at the site that I could not put my finger on. I brushed it off thinking that I had been imagining things. But it kept surfacing. Something was not right! But what was it? I had noticed lately that whenever I arrived there the builder was not on site.

There was always some excuse as to where he had been. I decided to keep a constant check on him. He had been asking for money more frequently, saying that he needed to purchase materials. I had no choice other than to rely on his integrity and place my complete faith in him. However I resolved to spend more time at the site and started the landscaping and planting lawn

## LETTER FIVE

*Blessings to you Beverly,*

*Many thanks for being an instrument, these short notes give Pam so much upliftment, and I thank you and your guides. Your sister Ruth is a tough one. (Beverley's guide)*

*My Dearest One,*

*I love you and wish to be able to express this universal love for you. I often embrace you and put a warm light of protection around you. You never have to fear the physical. I am near. We do have so much to do together and I am guiding you from this side. I love the 'surprises' you get, so not everything is told to you in readings, and know that when you get these surprises they are my gift to you, to enlighten and uplift you. To see you with your arms encircling the 'little one' is pure delight and I can sense the healing taking place.*

*Even though you long for my physical presence, I am always there. Just reach out. Actually reach into the air around you. I am there, sharing your every special moment. When others let you down I am there. Take care of yourself my little one. You do need to rest up a bit more. You are about to enter a new level of experience.*

*You will find that there will be stronger spiritual force present in your life, causing your perception to increase. I am so proud of you and the progress you have made.*

*Love, and love you for always. Allow me to write to you. I need to express my depth of feeling for you, as only you will understand.*

*Raymond*

Charlene had just given birth to her third son, 'Cody'.

## LETTER SIX

*Dearest Love,*

*I have been constantly with you. You look so precious when you sleep my Darling. I am guiding you constantly and feel so much love for you. You will always have my eternal love, light and soul. We are the true elements of soul mates and there is an eternal bond, which cannot be broken. I send out constant rays of love to you, that I know you feel. Things will soon take a swing for the better and there is a great deal of importance attached to the 27th of August. Watch out for the one who calls herself Margo. She is not going to be loyal to you. Adam and Carl will need your spiritual help. See what you can do my love. Not much energy this time but I want to send you a message of re-assurance and tell you of my constant love and devotion to you. I love and adore you.*

*Love, love and love you.*

*Raymond*

The 27th of August was the day that I received payment from the Compensation Office. Carl had been a good friend of Ray's. Adam was a young man who had pleaded to me for guidance, as at that stage I started to do readings and give spiritual guidance to people who could not cope with their lives. Many who had suffered loss would contact me and I was amazed at the communication channeled through.

*My Darling One, Creature of Love and Light,*

*Well! I said to Beverly today! No more writing! You know how I hated to write! It's so long and labored and drawn out, and why bother when I am a 'whiz' at the computer, hey?*

*Well there is so much more energy and light around you my darling, that I am constantly drawn to it and so re-assured by it. I am so very happy at the outcome of the case. You always knew it would just be a matter of time for I wouldn't have let it rest! Believe me my pig headedness remains in spirit too. It is difficult for me to stay in spirit and see you struggle in the material world. Here, there is no need and everything is energy and projected in thought. You only have to think of something to have it projected right before you!*

*And how often I wish I could pass this energy onto you in the horrible material world in which you exist. We have a plan, to work together for eternity my love and it will always be so. I will never for one moment leave you and am ever close. You will find that you are experiencing a kind of strange feeling, like not quite being in the world or having your feet on the ground and this is because you are going to experience a shift in your current consciousness. All aimed at your spiritual growth and development. I am SO proud of you my only little one! We have meetings here too. No one is one but each a part of a whole and you have so many credits. We call you 'an angel of light' and you are 'an earth guide' reaching out to others and making the way for the 'spirit guide' so much easier. You work with us daily.*

*There is no special message I wish to give about anyone this time, as there are no major problems around. I look at you with the little one and see so much joy. I am part of it too. I send out all my love to you in the universal sense Know it is not just my arms wrapped around you but my whole universal energy. I flow around you, in you, through you.*

*'Nti' - There is a letter for you in safety, I can't say why, please work it out, time to go.*

*All my love and entire being,*

*Raymond*

From Bev:

*this is weird I don't know how to underline, have tried for ages, now from nowhere the underlining has come and I can't find where to put it off!!!! And he was so calm and chatty and full of humor and then suddenly a completely different focus. I felt panic, almost urgency, like someone trying to get a coded message out, and this underlining? Don't know what? And there is no energy there now. Sorry I can't explain!! And now how do I get rid of this line!! Love Bev. The line just went! I swear to you! I never touched a thing on this computer! I just got the urge to add a P.S. to it before I printed it, to say that I'm certain it is the same energy, in other words Ray did not leave and some other guide take over. This has really spooked me!! I swear the line came and went on its own!!! I was just wondering how I was going to do other readings today with the line there. What is it all about?*

*Love Bev.*

The case referred to was in fact, the compensation case, but up to now I have not recovered the letter or found out what" Nti" means.

Ray loved the computer and spent many hours on it at home. I used to call it "his toy" I could understand his frustration at having to write by hand. He was managing somehow to still use the computer after all.

## LETTER EIGHT

*Dearest One,*

*I am so happy to be granted this communication with you. Although you do know that I am with you daily, every moment of the night and DAY!! And yet you seem to need confirmation of this through these notes, and so I give into your requests!! KNOWING that you feel me and listen to me at all times. There is so much I want to say to you. About how much I love you and how our love has no barriers to the physical. We are in tune spiritually and mentally. What more can I say?*

*You know I was never one for verbal expression, gave it all to you through my touch and need for you. I love you and am so proud of you and all that you have done!! You knew that you would have to stay behind and agreed to do this unselfishly, putting the needs of others beyond your own. I am here waiting for you. We will be together. We are now! Only the physical realm separates us.*

*Beverly is asking me to tell you more about the policy. It is in my name registered under NCI 22970. The broker has the number and should be able to look up information pertaining to this. You are noted benefactor. Everything else is going to turn out fine in the areas of financial issues. Just remain alert for a little while longer. Ask me when in doubt, I will answer. It's good to see you so relaxed and your laugh is like music to my soul. I feel drawn to the group. It's strange how wonderful a dead man is!! I laugh at the good words said about me, when Eric and I had our major disputes!! The energy is low and I take it as time to go!!*

*I Love you for eternity. For always,*

*Raymond*

I found the broker! They did have a policy with the number NCI 97202. Strange! The same numbers that I had been given in Ray's writing but they were reversed - Mirror Image? I was informed that the employer had allowed the policy to lapse! I felt uneasy about this and suspected that information was being withheld from me.

## Letter Nine

*Dearest One,*

*Thanks for the continued love and inspiration that I receive from you, it means so much to me and I can't thank you enough for getting the family together. Only you could have managed a mission like that, the energy and vibration was wonderful.*

*This letter may be stilted but I was never good at putting pen to paper and more so now, but I need to communicate with you. Never doubt that I write through you and enjoy that so much, as my energy blends with yours and emotionally I can loosen up and let you know how much I love you and how that love bonds through worlds. At times we are one, always the link, ever strong! It was my time to go and I have evolved along my spiritual path but I still have regrets. I would have liked to be more prepared but that was not to be and thanks to your energy I accepted quickly.*

*You know how I always had a plan, and everything had to work according to it. So, when I passed over I was angry, very angry. This was not how I planned it. But I will not progress any further until my Darling you are secure and have no more worries.*

*I still feel so bad at being so gullible, so trusting and drinking in all the promises of material wealth and great things when my greatest thing was YOU.*

*There was so much to be gained with me out of the way. I didn't even suspect the two men until it was too late. I greeted them in friendship and trust and wondered at the silence, until I saw the gun too late! And I knew I was prepared. I lifted immediately into spirit and "flew" to be at your side. You knew even then that the energy between us was so strong. You cannot hate, they were working through their own karmic paths, and there is no going back, only forward. I can wait until we are reunited and I promise you never to be parted again.*

*Raymond*

I could not believe this! What was he saying! Who did this to him? It was obvious that somebody he knew had murdered him. It had to have been someone that Ray had worked with!

Yes! Ray always had a plan. He was the most methodical man I had ever known.

The family re-union! His brother Donald and his wife Cindy, Norman, his brother and his wife Melanie, had come to visit me at the South Coast. There was no doubt that Ray had been there with us.

Bev called me to say that she had been very concerned when this writing had come through. She sensed that Ray was very emotional and that he ended very abruptly. I was really saddened by this as I felt that he was not settled and asked her to try next time to ask for names.

## LETTER TEN

*Dearest One,*

*I know that you are feeling so low and empty and frustrated. I am still me. I have lost nothing of the essence of me, or the love I feel for you or the hopes and dreams. We are one and in that oneness, at peace. I loved you from the moment I saw you and want to thank you for all the love and support you gave me and the times we shared, it strengthened me in times of weakness and comforted me in my times of sadness. Thank you especially little one for all that YOU taught me, for I doubt I could ever have achieved so much without what you did to help me free myself from the shackles of my past and give me so much spiritual growth when I needed it most. It's true that I also feel down and blue now, not much time we shared and yet so many memories that even now make me laugh and cry. I try to help in so many little ways daily and am always so thankful for this opportunity, but whatever I give is so less than what you have given me. I know that you are frustrated, and demand retribution for my passing. I am not at liberty to give names. Beverly has asked me too, but we have to work by universal laws and to EVERYTHING there is a reason and a season.*

*Events will work out as they are planned. I can tell you that soon the truth will be revealed and much will come to light. I was able through writing, to get the wheels in motion. They are turning, please be patient for just a little longer my love and all will be clearly revealed. I have been very busy in advancement of my soul progress, and it is a great privilege to still be allowed to remain so close to you. I am able to tune so easily into your thoughts, and merger so easily into your vibrations, that there is really no need to communicate in any other way, but I know you need to have some solid link at times.*

*So, here I am in this form. I love you now, and always, for infinity. Share the peace I feel and feel me always in your dreams, your hopes and future plans. Have faith in the universal workings of cosmic law.*

*I adore you, love always, forever,*

*Raymond*

## Letter Eleven

*Dearest One,*

*I am always so grateful for these brief moments in which I can re-assure you that I am with you constantly. I will see that no danger comes to you, you have a guardian angel in me and I will guide you to the best of my ability. I am very limited in what I may or may not do, for you see my love, you are still living your lessons and I am not allowed to interfere with karmic laws or lessons, which are yours to learn. All I can tell you, is at present you are being tested, you have to act on your faith and the inner certainty that I try to give you that everything will be okay. Faith and complete trust are needed now. I will not allow any unnecessary harm or hurt to come to you. You will be making a major breakthrough with 'the girls' soon.*

*I know how much this means to you and you are so close. Don't ever doubt yourself. You know that you are closer than ever before. I will be there to share your joy at the breakthrough. Also matters concerning me will be resolved soon.*

*Within the next two months you will hear some new evidence that will come to light as they establish contact with an African man, the one who had the unusual features, almost an 'East African' look about himself. So concern yourself with this matter no longer. You have opened the necessary doors.*

*One of the girls is here and assists you too. You swell my heart with pride at the help you give others. I love and adore you, as you know!! For eternity! Our energies are forever together in the universe. I could write words and words about our universal love but you know all that and I am with you always. I will from time to time try to get a little note to you, mainly for your upliftment, as I know you need these little re-assurances!!!*

*Love you now, always and forever,*

*Raymond*

## LETTER TWELVE

*Dearest One,*

*There seems to be some time for me to say a few words to you, you seem to be so low and down and it is hard for me to get through to you when you are like that. Darling, you need to work in silence – In the silence you will know me. Your efforts and hard work are coming to fruition and you will see the rewards, I promise that.*

*There is much movement beneath the surface that you cannot see, subtle shifts and changes. Silence is your greatest weapon now, it unsettles Heinrich terribly, he does not know what to expect, keep it up my love. You will hear progress soon. Tell Carl, hi! You take care little one. I am always there for you and your guiding light. Be happy. I dance in your radiant light. It energizes my whole being. Until later, I am with you always. Trust in the comfort you bring to me.*

*Always and forever,*

*Raymond*

Although I had constant communication from Raymond I still missed his physical presence so much and found it difficult to live between two worlds. I believed in the after life and knew that I should not grieve for him, as by doing so I was preventing him from evolving and continuing on his spiritual path, but still found it too painful to accept.

## Letter Thirteen

*Dearest One,*

*How I enjoy my precious moments with you. You only have to ask and I will be there. Bev may have found it strange that her reading didn't follow the usual tarot lines and that is because it's got a good part of what I want to say in it. See the picture of what I say, it will manifest as will the gift of sight, for I know that is what you are truly waiting for my darling, and it will be so, I promise. How many times have you seen my shadow and then doubted your active mind and your imagination?*

*Well doubt no more. I am progressing on my spiritual path here too and it is wonderful because you still work alongside me. We have so much work to do my love. You also need glasses to go with the granny image. You know what I mean! See to it! If only you can see what I can, the fast growth in all areas, you are moving forward very quickly.*

*NO DOUBTS NOW!!! The wheel turns slowly, but it does turn and that was always your fault, 'impatience', but soon, very soon, there are going to be some fast moving developments and a lot of excitement. Tell my brother to stop procrastinating and get on with it. By the way the swing needs fixing too. Darling love, I could talk for an eternity about my love, love and love for you, it surrounds you constantly, each moment of your life and my heart swells with pride, devotion and love for you.*

*Always now and forever yours, all my love,*

*Raymond*

I had in fact lost my reading glasses and was waiting for a new prescription to arrive, hence the remarks about my eyesight.

April 1$^{st}$ 1999. Finally the builders had moved off and I could move into my new home. For two and a half years I had been busy with this project.

After experiencing one problem after another, being conned by contractors who stole money and then building materials. It seemed that every single contractor, whether it be, the builder, the plumber, or the carpenter, had let me down in some way, which ended up causing law suits and costly delays with the building. Had it not been for the spiritual guidance that Yvonne and I had received we might have given up. But finally, against all odds, we had made it.

We were able to laugh about it as Yvonne and I could imagine the frustration that Ray and Bert must have felt, both having been in the building industry. So many times, for the duration of this project, I was given some intuition that something was going on, and then I would immediately drive over to the site.

I knew that I was being guided and my intuition was always correct. I would walk around and discover whatever it was that I had been "sent" to investigate. Once again I had to dismiss another contractor as he was transporting our building materials to another project that he was building. Our patience and our faith, it seemed, had been tested beyond the limit.

As I began to arrange my furniture, I felt Ray's loss so deeply. He should have been here to share this beautiful place. He should have been here to help me. I did not know where to start. The emptiness was just too much to bear. I received a fax from Bev the next morning, once again confirming that Ray could feel what I had been experiencing. I only had to ask and the answers were given to me.

## Letter Fourteen

*Dearest one,*

*Don't lose sight. You are so close to your goal. I love and adore you and you know that, a universal bond binds us together, so my progress is yours and yours mine. You have sensed the urgency of me wanting to talk to you. It's only that I am saying don't give up. Many changes are taking place in your life. Don't resist them for they are actually progressive. I love the light of the candle and as it glows you will see me. Your arrangements of the home are lovely, but move the chair to the right. It will look better.*

*The picture in the room is not straight. I moved it for you. I try so in little ways to show you that I am still around, so never doubt that. I know I sound real serious, but you do need so much re-assurance now and that's my main purpose today. To show you I am still part of your life, in so many little ways, others might think it crazy, that a 'spook' will come back and tell you how to arrange your furniture, but I know that's what you need right now.*

*It's the only re-assurance that I can give you. Look after yourself more. Remember your low energy will affect my ability to communicate.*

*I love you for all time,*

*Raymond*

Although I was now used to Ray's, writings, this was so amazing. Just when I needed him the most, he was there!

Raybert Lodge was on its way. I had already started to receive calls from desperate people who had suffered the loss of a loved one, from all over South Africa. I was able to communicate with whom they had lost and set their minds at rest. My ability to do readings telephonically being a "clairaudient' made it easier to help so many more people and reach out to others who were unable to call on me.

Information was being channeled through to me while I spoke to them on the phone. I could feel that my psychic powers were increasing and was totally in awe at the information that I was being given. One particular incident comes to mind. I had received numerous calls from a woman who told me that she had lost both her son and her husband within three months of each other and wanted me to communicate with them.

I explained that I could not 'just call them up' when I chose to, but should they want to communicate with me they would come through. I could not pick up anything and I knew that she was bitterly disappointed.

When she called again a few days later, I happened to be extremely busy at the time and began to tell her that I could not help her, when all of a sudden I saw two men! I began to describe their appearance to her, and managed to establish that this was in fact her late husband and son. I found myself in front of a house and began to describe it to her with amazing clarity.

It seemed that I was being taken on a tour of the entire house! We went from room to room as I spoke to her on the phone, describing furniture and archways etc. Although she had called me from her business she told me that I was in fact describing her home to her. I was then taken into her son's room where I was able to describe the blue curtains, his radio tape deck and all the little things that he treasured.

I was able to give her messages that meant so much to her. This was to be the beginning of her healing process as she was overjoyed at the news that she had been given.

Every so often I would experience these startling visions and I began to wonder if there was a purpose attached to them. Why would I be shown through a house? As usual when asking a question in my thoughts, Ray was always around to give me an answer. "You need confirmation at times my love, so do not doubt the information and directions that we give you regarding the missing girls".

Ray had promised me while he was alive, that he would find a way to help me solve this mystery, he had kept his promise. I knew that he would never let it rest until the case was solved, even if it meant him doing it from the afterlife.

## LETTER FIFTEEN

*Dearest One,*

*Help is on the way. Things will improve shortly. Life is about to take on a greater purpose and meaning. I only write to you through Beverly's vibrations because she can be trusted and is not one to ask for public attention and is completely trustable. Be aware that I only write to you through her to give you confirmation of all that I give you. Be wary of those who seek to take credit from you.*

*Don't trust those so-called psychics that only seek self- gain and attention. I feel so frustrated in your search. People say that they want some proof. They want something concrete but we have given then all that and they remain closed to all the facts. I will continue to guide you in the direction that you need to go, energy is low but I am beside you at all times Precious One,*

*Raymond*

I had been helping the crime unit once again to search for the missing girls. Ray was disappointed, as again the search had come to an abrupt ending.

## LETTER SIXTEEN

*Dearest One,*

*I am thankful for the opportunity to tell you how proud I am of you and how I adore you. Darling One, you know you have suffered a loss again, but the universe knows best. Your little one has not passed over but is lost from you. He is in a family and well cared for and very happy. The little boy he is with has a greater need than you, love! It sounds cruel but you know how universal laws apply and you love, have to let go. There is just too much for you to accomplish, you have great spiritual guidance and protection and you can feel our love and protection of you dear one.*

*You are well loved. Your work on the girls has caused big waves and there is a lot of movement there, you are on the right track! Keep the pressure up. Could go on and on and on and on! I am with you always, now and in eternity. You are blessed and will attract good things to you. David sends his love too. I am doing well in my progression but await YOU! I waited too long for you and our time was too short, but we now have eternity ahead.*

*Love always,*

*Your Raymond*

My little Dog Digby, fondly known as ‘Diddle Dum’, had been missing for two months. I searched everyday, walking on the beach, scouring the bushes close to my home. I advertised, checked regularly at the S P C A. and phoned the local vets constantly. I placed photographs of him at every shop and supermarket, hoping that somebody would bring him back. He was my constant companion and I could not bear to lose him. When I read Ray’s message I was horrified. Why should I suffer another loss, The S P C A had hundreds of dogs who desperately needed good homes, why should I lose ***my*** little one? Eventually I began to accept, after all, he was a special little soul and yes, perhaps this little boy needed him. I began to understand that one of the most important lessons that I have to learn in this lifetime is ‘Acceptance’. After all that is why we are here. We have chosen to come back and rectify our karma and even though I do follow the spiritual path I do still have many lessons to learn.

## Letter Seventeen

*Dearest One,*

*Soon there is going to be a happy re-union, do not worry. You need to be positive, you are sending out a guiding beam and soon there will be joy. You will also see the reason for why events have happened the way they did. Do not get so logical. Remember the test of faith. Your energy level is high and so the answers you seek will come to you in the natural light of day. I am beside you always. Keep happy, the outcome is positive and you know what a straight talker I am!! Seeking is going to give you new clues as to the girl's disappearance. I told you there would be a development aimed at you, be alert at all times. I love you and am always close at hand, so never despair!! I will make contact again soon. I only want to re-assure you.*

*Love forever and in eternity.*

*Raymond*

## Letter Eighteen

*Dearest One,*

*I am so grateful for the times I get to communicate with you. I love and adore you and live through you. A lot of changes are about to occur to you and these will make you feel the effort has been worth it. Public attention and acclaim comes to you!! Well Done! I am so proud of you my heart is bursting. Home is your refuge. Tell 'Piet' to slow down, his health is not too good at present.*

*There is about to be a new development with the girls. You must write all your impressions down from the first moment of contact. It will form a pattern and give you greater insight, it will later be published. One of the 'girls' says there is a celebration soon and she feels sad because she was murdered and cannot rest until her parents know the truth. She says the men were very cruel and they are still involved. I really wish that I could tell you more my love because you are so close to finding the answers. There is also going to be a new little soul coming to join your family. I love and adore you and am continually at your side giving you encouragement. You receive strong spiritual vibrations from a higher level than most, that's why it's pure thought forms. We are evolving together.*

*Love for eternity,*

*Raymond*

I began to learn how to use a computer and could not understand why it would bring up programs without me touching anything. The screen would flicker and change colour. Before I could rectify a sentence, it would change in front of my eyes. Sometimes I would write a paragraph, which was obviously not correct, and look up to see the screen was a dark pink, but when I rectified the error it would change back to white. Soon after, I received this writing from Bev.

## LETTER NINETEEN

*Greetings Dearest One,*

*I do so love and adore you. Do not worry about the computer. It's only picking up on your vibrations, which I have told you! You are on a very high level. Both you and I work on a much higher and very fast moving energy vibrations beyond earthly perception, so don't worry, it will come right. It's just that the vibration level around you is very high, as we have been sending energy into you.*

*You have been astral traveling with us and you learn and gain extra knowledge and understanding. If you went for a medical check up you would be surprised at the low pulse rate that you have because you are working on a very high spiritual vibration. You are much in control because of all this energy. You will also be finding that objects appear and disappear before you, again it is the high energy level of vibrations. I have an American Indian guide, (its more Guru) with me. He is helping us to meet our goal and gives us lots of assistance, although you are often wary, or even scared when you sense his energy around. But he is your protector and quite a serious fellow. I call him Gerald and it's a joke that has stuck.*

*Your continued love and perseverance in spite of your difficulties, gives me so much upliftment and inspiration. Your faith is wonderful! And we marvel at your ability to cope. What you give out enriches you each day. You will gain threefold. We have a surprise for you in November so hang in there. You are like a beacon of light to spirit beings too.*

*There are alien creatures too and they will make contact with you as you are on the same vibration, but you have nothing to fear. Realize my love that you do exist on a different vibration level to others. You are more Spirit! The universe knows what you are in need of and is producing. I love and adore you now and always. Eternity is ours.*

*Yours always,*

*Raymond*

## Letter Twenty

*Dearest One*

*Seems like we have a communication problem this side too! An 'engaged' signal all night and you know how my problem is with that! Darling, things are going to move quickly for you now. You will be amazed at how our plans are all coming together. You had to let go of so much, but nothing is ever in vain and this is the only way the plan can work as you are being used as a signal, a beacon for fellow travelers. They will need friends as they become more and more a reality.*

*They are good elements, their technology needed in order to protect future generations. You are right to predict an event that will soon happen in Egypt. Don't be scared because you have a high spiritual protection around you. You have been put through a series of tests and come out tops. I am so proud of you, as all here know. Because of that, our earthly link and bond is allowed to remain strong. You are doing a lot of astral traveling with me so you must try to have a short rest and renew your energy during the day. Well love, no great revelations to impart. Just know that now and always we are together, never apart.*

*I adore you always, eternal love,*

*Raymond*

Bev told me that she had been on the phone for quite a long time and it was obvious that Ray was really frustrated at not being able to get her attention. Her computer had also been down and I knew that this would prove to be very annoying for Ray, as he had begun to communicate more frequently since both Bev and I started to use computers. Often when she was sitting down to e-mail she would feel Ray was around and that there was an urgency to write. He would begin immediately which meant that Bev could send it straight on to me.

## LETTER TWENTY ONE

*My Darling Pamie,*

*I have the computer working like I told you I would. It is a far easier way of communicating. You have felt the build up of the new cycle and energy around you. You will be amazed at the developments over the next few weeks.*

*Your spirituality is also going to increase and there will be much more work for you to do. I remain close to you at all times. You will be overjoyed at the news you will have from Pat and your focus will become clearer. Susan is going to take a fall but it will not be as bad as it seems so you know to encourage her as you usually do. Yvonne must take care as there is a dangerous element around her, but not for long, it remains there only for a short spell but your powers are stronger and will overcome this. BUT!! She does need to have protection. Place salt around her home and place her self within a white light in the mornings and evenings. You are about to have powerful recognition as your predictions surface.*

*Cover- ups are clearly indicated but your efforts have not been in vain. I am constantly at your side and give you loads of energy. You feel when I am there and perk up just like you always did. I love the sparkle in your eyes and the laughter in your voice. Don't ever lose that.*

*Love you now and for eternity,*

*Raymond*

Before I received this writing I had noticed whilst doing a reading for Yvonne that there was danger surrounding her and had warned her that she should not go to work for a few days. Being the sheriff of the entire area, she would be exposed to very dangerous elements. She had lost her husband in the same manner and was not about to take any chances. As a precautionary measure, she employed a security guard at her office. I was amazed at Yvonne's faith and belief. I could sense after a few days that the danger had passed and let her know that she would be fine. During that period there had been an element of danger as she had been forced to attach a vehicle from a man who had become violent and threatened her life.

As Ray had predicted, I received a call from Pat. She had lost a valuable ring and was devastated. The ring was of great sentimental value to her and she wanted to know if there was any way that I could help her to find it. Pat had been out doing landscaping and thought that she had lost it in one of the gardens.

She had searched the entire day, retracing all her movements; gardens that she had worked on, including going back to a restaurant that she had been to on that day, but could not find it. I told her that I could sense that she had a pale blue bedspread over her bed, with a fringe around the edge. She confirmed that she had. The ring, I told her, had caught on the fringe of the bedspread and was now lying on the floor close to a cupboard. She phoned me a short while later, elated because she had found it exactly as I predicted. I knew that these little incidents were to encourage me and help me to focus more on the work that I was now to do.

Another prediction that came true - One of my clients had lost some really important documents, which were the only proof he had to verify ownership of a property, which belonged to him overseas. A previous partner of his it seemed had registered the property in his own name.

At that stage my client was living in South Africa. I told him that he would find the documents in a dark room, which looked like an attic, in a manila envelope, in a suitcase. I also mentioned that I could see he would immigrate to the UK. He knew nothing about that but would begin searching his house for the documents.

He searched and searched in his home, almost turning the entire place upside down but could not find them. He eventually gave up and did in fact immigrate to the UK. I received a phone call from his ex wife a few months later to tell me the good news. Dick had decided to go and visit his sister outside of London.

When he arrived she told him that some of his things, which had been brought over from their late father's home, had been stored up in her attic. Would he like to go through them to see what he needed? There in this dark attic, in a suitcase, in a manila file, he found his missing documents!

## Letter Twenty Two

*Dearest One,*

*Firstly I must say that there was a big shift around your environment. Issues are being resolved in your favour. Your intuition is so strong so be guided by it. Your contacts are getting stronger, as you grow and astral travel too. You are given the knowledge and insight to take back because you use it wisely and for no self- gain or ego advancement. Life will never be routine or settled for you as you have so much to accomplish. But as I said before, you are more spirit than physical because you are lifted to my vibration level. Tell Donald to hold with any investment until March because he will get a clearer picture and he must get his vehicle repaired.*

*He is always putting off for tomorrow what needs to be done today. Tell Norm I had a good laugh at him and to lighten up some.*

*Love, love and love you now always and for eternity.*

*May your guiding beam reach out to all, and my love you are blessed always. We don't need physical touch. Our bond goes beyond all earthly expectations and understanding. Believe in YOU and ME and most important, in us eternal.*

*Yours always,*

*Raymond*

Bev had come to visit me. In all this time of knowing her and receiving the wonderful messages from Ray, I had only seen her once when I had gone to her for a reading. She is an extremely busy person and usually booked up for months at a time for readings.

I knew how exhausting this work could be, as I was also busy with readings and giving spiritual guidance and support to an 'ever growing' list of clients. Occasionally we do need to take time out for ourselves to replenish our energy. I managed to persuade her to come and stay at Raybert Lodge to have a break. It was wonderful to sit and relax and enjoy the beautiful surroundings.

Bev went off to her chalet to have a rest and was back a short time later. “Ray is not going to let me rest!” she said with a smile. “He has got too much to say to you,” and presented me with pages of writing which had just come through.

## Letter Twenty Three

*Dearest One,*

*It's wonderful to listen to you talk, but you know that I know all the thoughts you have and we are so closely bonded that I know your thoughts before you do. You seem surprised that I didn't comment, when it's nonsense you talk. There has only ever been one soul mate in your life and that has been me. The rest, well, that was just trivial matters and you getting to appreciate me.*

*I love you eternally, you are all mine, always before, during, and after my physical presence in your life. I have told you that I cannot answer questions and won't even answer when you yourself know. You have the answers within you.*

*Everything in the universe has a set order, things happen as they are meant to happen and no knowledge I can give you about Heinrich, will bring his payback time any closer. Also My Darling, you are not to be the instrument in which his downfall will come from. We are keeping your energy pure.*

*To get you to execute revenge on my murderer would call for karmic debt from you and so part our link. So he will have his fall, but not from any evidence or help from you. One evil act does not call for another of revenge.*

*I know that you would feel so much better but that is not part of the plan and even though you will deny this now, one-day, you will look him in the eye and say that you forgive him. It is the way you will go. For my murderer the saying does go 'The higher you climb the harder you fall' and his fall will be tremendous. I don't like to say too much because that only fuels the anger you have inside.*

*I say, 'let it be' for a time. You have the answers. Why did he phone you? Because he knew that his deed was done!! They met him and collected the money from him and drove the car out for him, he was also close enough to hear the shot but not witness the actual shot, but it is done and he is in great mental stress. It will be revealed. You need not fear that. Everyday he lives in fear and is so scared of death. Enough now! You have the answers so don't ask again. You are not going to 'used' as an instrument in this! Stay Pure! Let the universe sort it out.*

*Yes I do wear a blue robe now, as you start the spiritual spiral of knowledge, you progress into robes. New souls and souls progressing first wear white! You my love put on a white robe as you travel into astral.*

*You shed your earthly clothing and put on the White Celestial Robe as a form of protection and also purity, as you guide others to the light. I have progressed to blue, the colors of healing and clairvoyance and therefore able to give you healing. I often place my hands on your head or shoulders, especially when you sit at the computer and I am far more 'clairvoyantly' linked to you now than ever before.*

*The writing you will be doing is going to be writings that we will be sending you. This is knowledge that will come to you and you will call this book 'LETTERS FROM RAYMOND'. It may take years in the process, but it will be. Sweet One I have little time left and I think all your questions are answered and you have the answer within your heart.*

*I love you eternally. Yours always,*

*Raymond*

Yes! The thoughts that I was having and the questions I was asking had been answered. I knew that I would now have to accept that there was nothing more that I could do regarding his murder. It had been eating me up inside but I had to let it go and move forward.

I had been talking to Bev about my wonderful relationship with Ray. I had compared him to others I had known before he came into my life and was really amused at his remarks. I was being gently reprimanded.

I had also had known that I was to write a book, as the lessons and messages being sent to me were such an important universal link. They could not possibly have been intended for me alone, so many people would benefit from them being published. I was also made aware that when the time was right, it would happen. I had no doubt that I would receive the help and guidance that I would need to complete the task.

## LETTER TWENTY FOUR

*Dearest One,*

*There are many developments taking place. Be aware of them. There are new ideas taking place but you can be assured that you are getting closer and closer to your goals. We have been giving you a lot of spiritual healing and your energy level will soon pick up.*

*Poor Sweet, you work so hard in the astral but you have asked that you do not retain the memories, as it just would be extra worries that you don't need. You have a busy period coming up but don't worry because I will be there to guide you all the way. I know anniversaries and celebrations are a low point for you but I remain with you always. It's just that you still wish to feel on the physical, but already we meet on a spiritual vibration and experience all the joys we have always had. It's so good to be able to still share your life's cycle.*

*Do you know how rare and seldom that is granted? It's all part of the universal plan because without you there and me here, Spirit would never be able to achieve as much through you. I am progressing so much and a vast amount of knowledge is being given to you.*

*Only few have the privilege and we know you use it wisely. I do communicate with you every moment of the day and night we share in the astral, so really there is no need for writing. I do so only because I know it brings you so much joy and you do need some upliftment today. I wish I could give you more about the 'girls.' I have explained the laws of karma and cause and effect. Some things on the earth plane need to work to time. They need the prayers to help them from that dark place. Much is going to come to light and new clues are emerging.*

*I will like it when I get back to the computer. How are the tricks? Gives you something to think about! The answers are available to those who seek. It is like a 'needle in a haystack', but you will find it!*

*Love, love and love you, always and eternity,*

*Raymond*

At this stage Bev did not have the use of her computer and had to write these by hand. I knew that Ray was having fun on my computer however, as all kinds of weird things were happening.

Words and sentences would change before my eyes. The screen would change colour, and bring up different programs without me touching anything! I was a little wary of this in the beginning but soon got used to it. I would switch the printer on to print a page and could not switch it off! It would start to print page after page of coded messages, similar to sacred writing.

This was happening on my computer as well as Beverly's and Yvonne's. I still have those messages and hopefully will find somebody to decode them.

## Letter Twenty Five

*Dearest One,*

*How lovely to see you smiling once more, your smile lights up your eyes, the seat of your soul. I know what an effort it is for you to smile when so often you feel the heaviness and heartache.*

*I'm amazed at the patience you have when you listen to the petty problems, when you yourself have experienced so much pain, but we are unique and joined eternally for now and forever.*

*Yes, I am giving you the information ahead of it happening in order to increase your confidence, because you are going to have to have a lot of inner faith, confidence and complete trust in what we are going to tell and reveal to you. Much of it will be beyond your comprehension. Things are moving very quickly and you will find that your efforts will not be in vain. Pressure has been increased on everyone. There is much movement and new openings and success.*

*It has been difficult to do this small piece of writing. Beverly has not been able to sit still, but I will soon write again and until then know I am with you always and our link is so strong. There are bigger plans for Raybert and I will reveal them soon.*

*Love, love and love you for always and eternity,*

*Raymond*

## LETTER TWENTY SIX

*Dearest One,*

*We are very busy at work in the astral as there is much preparation to do. Much noise is made about the new era that the world is moving towards. Yes it is moving into a new level of Spiritual Enlightenment.*

*The growth of this will be seen in some amazing way within the next five years. Those that currently exist on the material level will be left far behind as the material takes on less and less meaning. The new era heralds soul growth and development.*

*We are preparing the way for many souls who will soon pass over in order to make room for 'new enlightened beings'. Many of the souls passing over will have existed in the dark and will be difficult work for us. We have placed enlightened souls like yourself and Beverly in areas where they will be of great assistance to humanity and ease the way of acceptance of all that is to come.*

*Although the chosen ones have been preparing for this moment all their lives, they have come into this incarnation knowing of the enormous task they were about to take on. It is 'all fine' to do so in spirit, that is to accept such a huge task, and it was only the enlightened ones that this was available to. But even the Bible says 'the flesh is weak".*

*And so Dear ones, you are put through the most and greatest trials and tribulations, because not only was it to test your faith but also to give you the strength and courage to do the work that you have come to do. Of course as enlightened ones you feel different and alone and not part of this world. Well that is because you are not. It is not a coincidence that you are currently grouping and adding strength and support to each other, because this will be needed.*

*We have a plan and it involves the workers, as with you and Beverly. The task is huge, but we have built up a very strong support system for you, made up of enlightened individuals, whose support and help carry you through. This is just as important and our dearest Yvonne is one of those supporters. Her strength and assistance is wonderful. Do not think of it as cruel or unfair that you have all had to suffer so much. You took on the task, knowing the hardships, trials and tests. You have all come through them with A's and A+'s. Many of us in spirit rejoice at your achievement.*

*If wealth were measured by spirit, as is ours, it will be too in yours, a very short period of time before you became extremely rich. The bible says, "The Father has many mansions" and you will gain one of these. None of you are of this world so do not try to take on a worldly cloak. We will take care of all your material 'needs' and wants. Have faith. Do not long for the physical love or touch, for the spirit world beams down love upon you every day.*

*You only need one quiet moment to still yourself and feel the divine light upon you. Yes Beverly I have told Pam about an event that will happen in Egypt and she has it in her mind, but a chain of events will happen there. That is why Spirit used Mark to give you that message last night. I knew I would get through to you by using a means that would make you pay attention.*

*Sometimes you and Pam make it so difficult for us. Write down all the flashes of inspiration, even if it doesn't make sense at the time. Store the information and then put it together again and then go over it. So! Mark never talks to you? Bert always loves a joke and he was laughing so much at your reaction. He suggested Mark, and it was a good impact hey? Yes giving that message to John or Grant, they would have gone into a long philosophical talk about it and in doing so lost the impact as you and Pam so often do.*

*Mark walked in, delivered the message and walked out. You were amazed and even checked on the computer. Right!! So Pam, Mark walked into the room where Beverly was writing her book on the computer and said, "Did you know that on the 31$^{st}$ December, 3 Planets line up in Egypt right above the pyramids?" Having said that he walked out.*

*Yes they do and yes they cause a terrific energy and ignite crystals and rock forms, hidden deep within the hearts of the pyramids, thereby activating new energy and developments upon the planet. There could be a series of disasters occurring in the area of Egypt, but these are not because of the activation of the crystals, rather man made disruption and unresolved issues. But the ignition of the crystals and powerful energy begins when the planets are overhead the pyramids and goes on activating until there is a massive wave of energy.*

*When in May, five planets activate over the whole world, there will be a great spiritual awareness and growth, but also a passing of souls. Raybert will be a Spiritual Center and Retreat that WILL BECOME KNOWN WORLDWIDE! We WILL build a Chapel and a Conference Center because it will be needed! Raybert is on a very Spiritual line. Pam we want you to go out into the garden with your crystal, you will feel the swing and it will feel like it is drawing into the ground. That is where the chapel must go, for it will restore light, love and life, to so many souls.*

*The energy is getting low from Beverly and I say thank you to her and to tell her she is truly loved and blessed in Spirit and that her efforts are not in vain. And so My Darling One, my soul connection through eternity, the writing must end. But I remain with you always.*

*Love, love and love you,*

*Raymond*

Shortly after I received this writing I heard over the news that there had been a plane crash where hundreds of people had been killed. A few days later I heard of more tragedies - another plane crash and earthquakes. I felt drained and exhausted.

No matter how early I went to bed at night I would wake up feeling that I had not slept. My body felt as though I had been doing heavy physical work. I was also starting to experience visions of being in very remote places. I knew once again that I was been used for "rescue work" as often happened after a passing of souls. I seldom felt Ray around and understood that he was busy. It was to be almost a month before the next writing came through.

## LETTER TWENTY SEVEN

*I surround you with positive and loving rays of energy. You are my love, now always and in eternity, no matter what may occur in your current and physical existence.*

*Darling One,*

*You have to learn acceptance the Universal Principals. Natural laws and principals govern everything in the Universe.*

*To everything there is a reason and a purpose. To everything there is a reason and a season. Nothing is co-incidental. You are put in the right place at the right time. The right people are brought towards you for the right reasons at the right time so do not question what the Universe provides and also takes away from you.*

*For everything there is a higher purpose. You are in a karmic period and as in all karmic situations we in Spirit are not allowed to interfere. You have progressed such a long way Little One. You have learned the basic acceptance of circumstances, which so often seemed intolerable to you. But in doing so, you have made the way easier for yourself and for us. Yes you have been strong and have the inner strength, but for the work you are to do you are going to require much support. As I have told you previously that is why you are being put into contact with so many people who will be supportive of your efforts.....*

(Incomplete as Bev received a visitor and had to stop abruptly)

January 14th, 2000.

The Continuation of the previous writing came through from Ray

*Greetings and thank you for the time of yours I am using, as your energy level is low. I am only allowed a certain limit of your time and energy. Sister Ruth (Bev's guide) makes sure of that. Bless her! She is a great protector and provider for you and you are truly blessed.*

*Darling Pam, to continue...*

*Every relationship is unique. It's all part of a divine plan. No two relationships can ever be the same. Each relationship, every person, is necessary for your soul development to your soul evolution. You have to face challenges and especially, changes, you cannot be left to stagnate in one area of safety. Accept changes and embrace soul growth as it brings you closer to me.*

*Believe me my Love, we have such a Universal Bond that nothing can break it or come between us. In Spirit we exist in a very different world and we have no physical desires and have gone beyond illnesses of the flesh like jealousy, fear, anger and such like. We live on a pure vibration of love, peace and harmony.*

*It is not at all difficult that another person is being brought into your life for I can see the greater purpose and the karmic debt you owe to each other. Spirit is wise, they have brought in someone who will support you in every way and will be in total acceptance of me.*

*I will always be with you and it will take a very special kind of person to accept that. No love will ever touch our love, you will gain comfort and support in this new relationship and I give you all my blessings, all of my love, and support. I never want you to feel a sense of betrayal or guilt, for it is not so. You are really being directed into the right areas and then there is going to be a lot of sudden growth and development.*

*Acceptance is of importance. You are progressing and as with any progress, come's change. Our love is on a Universal vibration. Nothing will change that. You are the one living through the emotions and that is why it is so difficult for you. I am removed from the emotions and can see the purpose, the final plan! Spirit would not have guided you so far, only to have everything ruined by one man. He is of higher purpose.*

*It has been so difficult for me as I am always with you, but I am in Spirit and you are physical and still living out your karma. So you do need to have a companion!*

*Realize the purpose! Our world is so different, you have experienced it in the Astral, and I am here to guide you forward, never backwards. You worry that by forming ties with another I will go away. Not so! In fact, if you do not form ties with another, or lock yourself into yesterday, I will be forced to move on without you! For I would then be blocking your karma, holding your Spirit back from attainment, then all would be lost, because then when you did pass over you would be on a lower vibration and we would not connect. So accept and grow, for I do love you so, and nothing changes love.*

*Yours always, now and for eternity,*

*Raymond*

## LETTER TWENTY EIGHT

*Dearest One,*

*I bring light and love to you and greetings from the spiritual realm. We have been so busy as we told you in our writings there would be a passing of many souls and this is happening daily. Do not be troubled by it for it is all part of the destiny plan. We are preparing you for greater things. You do know this and are right to anticipate the movement around you. Raybert is about to become very established as was the plan and your rest period is almost over. Many blessings will be yours. Darling One, don't worry too much about our current slowing down of communication, for we are very busy and everything, in both our existence and yours, is very progressive. Jerry too will have a role in this new progression of developments.*

*He has a lot of healing energy and will be needed. He is aware of the developments and is accessing the changes it will bring to his life. Everything emerges when the time is right. You have already learnt the lesson of acceptance. Beverly has agreed to sit and take down the lessons we will start to impart to you from next week.*

*These you will be able to use in teachings and guidance. Just be wary, many people will like to share in or take credit for your glory. Remember always that they need you. You don't need them! Lessons can be harsh if learnt through experiences. That is why we will guide you. Use your pendulum for making decisions. I will work through that method. Norm needs to know that everything is okay and that I do often give him guidance in decisions but he often doesn't pay attention to the signs. He gets so darn logical, that he needs the earth shaken to believe! Tell him to relax.*

*It's good to hear you and Yvonne laugh and make future plans. Laughter lightens the atmosphere and it's so much easier to work directly with you. Happy birthday to my little man! I will communicate in length at a set time.*

*Love, love and love you. Yours in eternity,*

*Raymond*

## Letter Twenty Nine

*Dearest One,*

*Greetings to you from the spirit realm! Your path has been blessed. Do not feel apprehensive of what lies ahead, for there is much work to be done. You will be guided and directed to all the right areas. Events will open up so that they will be beneficial to your plans. As 'Osho' would say," Go with the flow" (Osho Zen was a Buddhist). We would never give more than you are capable of doing.*

*I know that Beverly is worried because she feels that other people are more learned because they have been on courses or have certificates, but that is not knowledge! True knowledge comes from the school of life, the experiences you have had.*

*You have both been though the school of life and you have the knowledge that no course or certificate could give you. That is why you feel the way you do about working in groups.....Because a group needs the support of others. Yet true Spirituality comes through self-growth and development.*

*Your skills and knowledge are earned, not just given by displaying a certificate. You have been schooled by life and guided by spirit. All the abilities and knowledge you need will come naturally to you, just as when you had your children.....you did not need a certificate to be a 'Mother'! It was a natural process. When your daughter fell and hurt herself.....you had no certificate to say 'Healer'!*

*It comes as a natural process. You washed, touched, kissed and bandaged it, 'natural', meant to be! Schooled by life! And in bigger things like Raybert, you will be schooled and the knowledge and gifts will come so easily to you. There is no need for high- sounding courses, certificates and weird and wonderful names!*

*People are drawn to you because you are so natural and are of them. No ego! No self-gain! Just working through your karmic course of guiding others! We need people like you to take people to the level of consciousness that then enables us to work with them. We will give you lessons that you will be able to use in giving others life, survival and knowledge.*

*There is much ahead, lots of activity taking place. There has not been much time for writing. Beverly was lead to read about 'Anam Cara'. It is such a brief word, but explains everything I have been trying to tell you in two little words. Not much time now...will continue shortly, love, love and love you.*

*Eternally yours,*

*Raymond*

Anam Cara: the celtic tradition has a wonderful understanding of love. The Gaelic word 'Anam' is 'SOUL' and 'Cara' is 'Friend"—'SOUL FRIEND'

*PART THREE*

# LESSONS

As Ray had mentioned in the previous writings, the lessons were about to begin. I was beginning to understand the purpose of this extraordinary communication and felt so privileged to be blessed with this wonderful gift. He understood that in order to continue with this work, I needed to heal. Until such time that I accepted his passing, I would never be able to do so. He gently guided me and supported me until once again I had the strength to continue. Raybert was finally complete and my true purpose in life was about to begin.

I had progressed on the Spiritual Path to such a degree that I no longer wished him back. I rejoiced in his transition and understood that there had been a purpose after all. The lessons that follow are simple universal laws to help us understand the reasons for being on this earth plane. Why each one of us chose to come back, and the lessons that we chose to learn?

So many people had begun to benefit from this divine help. It seemed so strange at first that as each new challenge was given to me by another desperate person, wanting answers after the loss of someone dear, a new lesson had already come through and I was able to set their minds at rest.

This enabled me to take them through their process of grieving, step-by-step. A support system had been formed and they in turn could hardly wait for the next lesson to be channeled through. To know that the person whom they had lost was actually still around made their loss easier to bear.

Often whilst I was talking to the bereaved little messages were channeled through to me, which meant so much to the person concerned. This in turn created a need for constant messages. I then had to help them realize that it was not possible to call up those in Spirit at my will, that the message that they had received was a blessing and confirmation for them to know that life is eternal, that death is only a transition.

It would be wrong for them to expect messages all the time, for their own sakes and for those that had passed over. Not all in spirit were in fact able to communicate. I began to receive hundreds of phone calls and endless requests for communication and messages. This drained my energy, for as much as I wanted to help, it was not always possible.

I could feel their pain and their sense of loss and desperately wanted to ease their burdens. I myself had been in a similar situation. The terrible void that one experiences after a loss is so hard to bear. So many people, saddened and desolate after the loss of a loved one, seldom fully recover.

In the beginning Ray had consoled me with personal messages. He gave me the courage to face the world again. I did not want to go on without him. But he wanted me to understand that although I had been helped in my time of sorrow, I too needed to move on, that the knowledge that I had gained through his writings and lessons, were intended for a very special purpose.

## *FIRST LESSON*

*Dearest One,*

*Well? Didn't we tell you that you that you would be busy! This is only the start of what we are preparing you for! As we told you before, Raybert will become internationally known as a Spiritual Center. Norm makes a lot of problems for himself because he is so logical and analytical - The thinker and the worrier. Just DO and the right situations will be provided. April is the time when he will see marked improvements financially, but he does have to work towards his goals and stop thinking!*

*As for you, My Love, you are protected and guided and never alone, for you are given higher inspiration and have the faith to go forward. I know at times it will feel like we are leading you forwards with a blindfold on, but its not so. All you need to know is that you are being led towards a higher purpose and by not knowing too much you can go forwards without and preconceived ideas. Heinrich is a very worried man. Did we not tell you that you didn't need to do anything? Bert would like you to find some time, as he needs to send a personal message to Yvonne via you. He says you will understand.*

*And with all that over I move on to the lesson for today:*

****Our world is so beautiful. You have no earthly words to describe the beauty or colours, or to explain it. I have to prepare you for these revelations slowly, but through these current writings you will be able to feel the pure energy, the beautiful vibrations, and most of all the Love. Beverly, in order to make easier contact we will ask that you secure yourself from interruptions and just relax as if in quiet meditation. Your thoughts won't affect the lessons and you will gain insight during this time into your own personal problems.*

*These lessons will serve a purpose and also as time goes by help you Pam, to understand why you are in flesh and I in Spirit. Knowledge is not gained in one sitting overnight, but with a system and great patience. The key however to all the lessons and to gaining greater understanding is 'LOVE'. Love is universal and felt by all, and so Dearest Ones, always give words of love, that is the greatest gift you can give.*

*Even if you do not understand the motives of another, give Love, Patience and Understanding, in order to turn the situation and the person around. EVERYONE responds warmly to LOVE. The greatest thing needed to work with us, is to accept and understand and get to know the Spiritual World around you without fear. Thoughts do have wings and whatever thought patterns you give out, you do attract towards you. So fear breeds fear, love and acceptance breeds love and acceptance. Your love and patience will be tried many times, but never let another's negative vibration turn you from the pure energy of Light, Love and Protection we have placed around you at this time. There is much work to be done, so many people looking for guidance and direction, and most of all, Peace of Mind!*

*They need to know that there is no such word as "Death". It is merely a phase, another cycle. A transition of one phase of life into the next! Acceptance of this transition makes the passing out of ones body into the Spiritual Realm a very welcome and happy event. The key word here is ACCEPTANCE. Life is a learning process and one that enriches the soul, so learn the lessons wisely.*

*Today the lesson has been a brief one and holds the key to understanding and that LOVE is Key. As you work with the spirit beings you will feel this pure energy and you need to spread that feeling as far as you can*

*Love, love and love you!*

*Eternally yours,*

*Raymond*

## *SECOND LESSON*

*Dearest One,*

*Beloved one, there is so much work ahead for you to do but I am always at your side and guide you and others in the right direction!*

*Life is an exciting journey to be traveled and enjoyed. May the Lord bless and guide you.*

*Here begins our lesson:*

*** *The world is currently at a turning point, new and combined energies are about to enter the atmosphere. Mans whole evolution and plan is quickening. You will notice this in babies being born, they have a 'wide awake' alertness right from the moment of birth and are special souls sent to take the world into its new age.*

*The energy is reaching out and establishing new attitudes in the heart of mankind. The world is entering a phase of great potential and all of this new energy is controlled by the mind. Although the world is moving into a cycle of great spirituality and 'outside' guidance, you already have many of them living amongst you in human guise and in areas of power and direction.*

*Each and every soul still maintains the element of free will, so although there will be those trying to guide you, and new laws to guide you, if you neglect to accept this guidance or obey universal laws, you cannot blame anyone but yourself.*

*Knowledge will be given to those seeking it. With this new energy, everyone will be able to have the gift of spiritual knowledge. The only limitations will be the limitations one place upon ones self. Most of the people progress to a point and then say 'I have found the knowledge' or 'I have found that which I seek' and remain there. BUT, there is always room for improvement and the soul quest is quite endless.*

*Even in spirit we never stop learning or progressing. To do so, is to stunt spiritual growth. Each person gets all the opportunities in life to liberate him self. The greatest liberation of the soul is to be able to free one's self from the constant wheel of life and death, and progress into the spiritual realms. Most of 'mankind' presently, live 'their' lives 'unconsciously', but they are moving into a more 'conscious' level of acceptance.*

*Many more will be finding 'their spirit' and thereby being led effortlessly into the new atmosphere and energy. There is no 'death', merely a swapping of 'Consciousness' - A transition into another realm of life. AND, by finding this spirit essence while on the earth plane, the shift and move of consciousness will be so much easier, and so too will the development of the soul. Be aware of soul consciousness all the time. This is done in simple ways, be conscious of your breathing, the very "energy" which keeps you alive. You do this daily, unconsciously, but to breathe is to live!*

*Be aware of this life force energy passing through you, by doing this you acknowledge it and by acknowledgement, this life force energy begins to work in a more positive way. Acknowledge all your senses, sight, smell, taste and touch. These too are lived unconsciously everyday!! Make them all part of your consciousness! By doing that, only then will you understand this lesson, so Dearest Love I leave you with much to think on.*

*Love, love and love you eternally*

*Raymond.*

## *THIRD LESSON*

*Dearest One and most beloved,*

*Yes I did say regular teachings would come through, but do not get logical about the hour or the day! We do not work according to your earthly timing of 24 hours and seven days a week! We work on vibration and environment energy!*

*So believe me the lessons are very regular! I tell the other guides that Pam will question everything and probe all that we have given in depth, because you would never accept surface values. Even now you still always question why? This is a good thing too. Yvonne will soon give you some good news about Heinrich, who is feeling very uncomfortable due to all the publicity.*

*Bert says to tell you he is working in the 'Arrivals and Departures' and he enjoys it so much. He never has much to say but was always a social person when he was in his earthly body, and he remains the same. Believe me, he forms quite a 'welcoming committee'! Time is advantageous to your plans and even more amazing and unexpected occurrences are about to occur, as you attract all that you need in the way of help and assistance.*

*Life is not always easy for you on the earth plane. However you are placed here to learn lessons. If you have not suffered then how can you feel compassion for the troubles of another? Try to think of life as a long, long journey, and all the turns you will have to make, perhaps even getting lost along the way, then how tired and discouraged you would be before you could even start the journey. Maybe you won't even attempt it!*

*Therefore take the journey of life one step at a time, enjoying each moment, savoring each experience, knowing that as you do so, you progress with each step, whether it be happiness or sorrow. The rewards awaiting you at the end of the journey are great. The world is a materialistic place. There are very few true spiritual people. Some people even become involved in such for materialistic or personal gain. So there are very few true mystical or spiritual people we can use as true channels for our work. God has given you both a gift and we need you both in order to channel our energy through.*

*By helping other people to deal with their problems is very important work, for you are able to guide and direct them onto the right paths and give them the means to channel the energy of the universe more wisely. We do not predict or lay down laws as to how people must live. Each one has free will and has to make his own choices or decisions in order to learn his own lessons and soul growth. The final decision is each persons alone, but we may channel and guide them through those who have a gift like yours.*

*Today's lesson is about colours:*

**** Colours play a very significant part in our lives, all of earth and universe has vibrations and everything has an aura of colour around. It may be a tree, a pebble, a plant, a chair or YOU!. These show many things about your level of spiritual attainment, your feelings and even your state of health. In spirit we too have auras of colours around us, as we progress we receive different colours to signify our level of our spiritual attainment.*

*How often have you heard someone exclaim, "Oh I just saw a flash of red!" or whatever colour? This is a 'spirits' energy or light you see. Progress in our realm is not forced, we are allowed to achieve at our own pace and levels. There are many lessons for us to learn here as well. It's true to say that one never stops learning. Very often some souls have to return to the earth plane to live as 'human' again and again, until they achieve the level of spiritual growth accepted here. This is why, first, many, many earthly lessons must be learnt and overcome before the spiritual ones can be searched for and attained.*

*Given with love and blessings. Darling Pam! Time to go now. Thank you for what you are doing and for reaching inside so many souls. Your efforts are not in vain and I work continually at your side. So much work to be done and so little time.*

*Love, love and love you. Yours for all eternity,*

*Raymond*

## *Fourth Lesson*

*My Dearest one and most beloved,*

*I am so proud of you and all that you have achieved and will achieve. I know at times that you question what is going to happen. But do know that all your plans are in accordance to the universe and so you will be provided for.*

*Don needs a bit of upliftment and he so enjoys hearing news from you. He is about to have a swing of good luck. Did you pick up that I want an apple tree? Apple blossom time! You know that you and Yvonne have been put on the same path! So it's not surprising that your cards and life paths will be so similar.*

*Today is the 9$^{th}$. In nine days time there will be surprising developments in Yvonne's life. You always amaze me Darling, at the positive energy you push into the lives of others even though you feel so alone. I wish at night you could just have a quick review of everyone you have touched, just for a moment and see how much, in a few minutes, you have changed around their lives and how they cope with the positive light you have given them to work off. You might feel it's all too much at times but you have merely put down the foundations and are at the beginning. You will be greatly blessed. Showers of blessings!*

*My love, we meet and communicate in the astral every night, as you are doing much rescue work, which is also a very important part that you play. So it is very important that you find time to rest in the afternoon, it's a real need! Or you will soon find your energy depleted. Its important for you to keep a journal of your ' dreams', for you are given much knowledge in the astral that you are bringing back, but retaining in the subconscious. All that comes to you in writing are all issues that we have discussed in the astral. That is why it always seems so familiar to you. My heart is so full of pride and love for you and it will always be that way. You have always given so much to me and now it is my turn to give to you. Life for you will be an adventure in every way. In past lives together we played the same roles of leadership and direction for others.*

*I wish you could see the higher purpose towards which you are working. But you already have the purest light and guides to work with who form a protection around you and Raybert.*

*As you have been dealing with the issues all week, the lesson tonight will be on death:*

**** That is the most important statement!! Death is a transition! An easy slide of one state of consciousness, to another! Transition is as easy as going to sleep and awakening to a more conscious state of existence. There is no need to fear death, for it is what you have been preparing for all your lives. You are sent to the earthly realm to learn lessons through experiences, and once you have learnt these you then progress to the next state or level of consciousness. Death relieves one of the shackles and limitations created in the body on a physical form. To fear death, is to fear the unknown, but it is such an easy transition from one state to another.*

*Birth is to be feared more than death!! All births create pressure on the soul and the body, and one is torn from the dark and safety of the womb to emerge into a human form, and from that moment of birth, take on karmic responsibilities and lessons. Life is a struggle even for those that seem to sail through it effortlessly. Death releases one from karmic lessons and repayments and is therefore a blessing.*

*On passing over, one is given the choice to either return or finish karmic responsibilities, or to rest the soul. This can take a few earth days to many earth years, depending on the individual involved. As with birth, death cannot be rushed forward or backward. There is a time to be born and a time to die. The greatest gift you can give yourself is one of acceptance. The universe and God know the divine purpose to which you are being led, so have faith, trust and acceptance. You will never be tested beyond your limits! You may feel that, but NEVER!*

*There is always a purpose behind the plan. As your soul passes into the new state of consciousness, there is such a feeling of divine love and protection. It's pure energy, a beautiful and perfect feeling of having returned home. And so, you watch over your loved ones left behind, with the knowledge of where life's course is taking them, and happy in the knowledge that they too will pass over in transition and join you in the realms of peace, love and enlightenment.*

*There are no earthly words to describe the pure energy and sounds of which you could not even imagine. So accept that life does have a purpose and that death is not an ending, simply a new beginning. May this lesson be Blessed.*

*Beloved One, I bless you and what you are achieving. Never fear, for I am constantly at your side and guiding you. I send people in to help you sometimes just in the nick of time, because you are often so quick to make a choice and you don't listen to my prompting! Then I have to send someone in quickly to save the day!*

*You do have a new Chinese Guide coming to work with you for a while. He was a very learned Doctor and will be using your energy to fulfill healing on those that you see. You have felt him around and he is short and wears white. He has a traditional beard and a long drooping mustache.*

*He is a very serious fellow and you have sensed his disapproval at times. You can acknowledge him by placing your hands together and bowing your head in greeting. He needs that acknowledgement. I have to leave now but I leave with all my love and blessings. To everything there is a purpose.*

*I love, love and love you.*

*Yours eternally,*

*Raymond*

I found this writing to be so amusing as I could imagine Ray's frustration when I instructed the builder to build retaining walls at the bottom of the bank instead of at the top, to prevent the storm water drains from flooding into the swimming pool.

We had so much rain that the pool had been submerged in mud four times within two weeks. Eventually I just stood there and cried out of sheer helplessness as I watched yet another mudslide would darken my sparkling pool. I decided to take some action and employed a laborer to build retaining walls. I had it all so beautifully planned and told him to proceed. The sooner the better!! Fortunately, a friend whom I had only recently met decided on his way home from work, to pop in and see me. He enjoyed our talks about the afterlife.

Errol called me on his mobile phone and asked whether I would mind if he called around for a short while. When he arrived I started chatting in my usual exuberant way. He interrupted me with a strange look, as though he were in a trance. "Show me where you are building the walls," he said. I found this to be really strange, as I had not mentioned anything to him at this stage.

I duly took him down and showed him what I was about to do. He explained that it would have been entirely wrong and proceeded to tell me how to go about it. He wasn't a builder and yet I knew once again that Ray had, in the nick of time, intervened, by sending somebody to see me and saved me from making what would have been a very costly mistake.

I had experienced a vision some months before, of this little Chinese man with the long drooping mustache, and was very intrigued as to why he was being shown to me in a vision. At last I knew the reason why and began to acknowledge him and greet him with the respect that was required. I began at this stage to concentrate on distant healing. I could feel him working with me. At times I would be so busy. I could receive between thirty and fifty phone calls in one day. I was concerned that I would not have time to do the healing that I had promised to do.

I need not have worried however, as I sensed my Chinese Doctor around, busy as always, looking after the people who had asked for help. I received numerous phone calls from people, amazed at the fact that they had been cured.

Yvonne had also developed healing powers, which were showing dramatic results. Often when I was really busy I would call her and give her a list of names. She would immediately get to work and pray for these people to be healed. Yvonne was of constant support to me. Her faith in the power of divine healing made it possible to help so many more people.

She had reached a stage whereby I could ask her to take calls from those who needed help and guidance. There were times when I too would almost give up from sheer exhaustion. I was receiving so many calls for readings and spiritual guidance. Although Ray kept reminding me to rest in the afternoons, it was not always possible. Yvonne was always there to encourage and uplift me.

I never had time to write things down into a journal as Ray had instructed me to do. I usually would tell her everything in our 'prime time' discussions, so she became my 'journal'. Things that I had long forgotten, Yvonne would remind me about at the appropriate time.

## *FIFTH LESSON*

*My Dearest Soul mate and most beloved,*

*I am always so happy to have the opportunity to deliver messages to you. It is your need not mine that makes a third party necessary. I do it to give you the acceptance that you are being guided into the right areas and I am always at your side directing you and guiding you.*

*Have you noticed at times of extreme stress or problems that befall you I don't seem to communicate through Beverly when you need it most? It's so hard to hold back at times like that my Darling, but as much as I would like to, I have to, as it is part of your own personal lessons. I cannot come in and give you all the answers.*

*But never doubt for a moment whether I am with you! I wipe away the tears before you can. You have shed so many tears, if you could look onto your lap and see where they have fallen, each little teardrop has formed into a beautiful crystal and each one with its own colour of light from the lessons you have learned. So there is just a glorious prism of light.*

*I am going quickly into the lesson for today:*

**** Parents are privileged in the knowledge that while in spirit their children themselves chose them, with the full understanding of the lesson they were to learn through their parents. They are only the image of their parents in appearances of the body. They have their own lessons to learn and karma to accept and live through. Life cycles are all about reaping from previous lives.*

*Children need to develop their own ways and have their own messages to impart. Learn to let their spirits be free, give love and guidance but learn too from what they are teaching you. Rekindle the joy in your heart by watching the keenness, awareness, the joy, the very trust of little ones and the joy in nature in being one with the universe and still so close to it. Little ones who pass into transition early are the true little angels of the universe. For them there is no such thing as death or fear, just tremendous joy and acceptance at being back in the beautiful place, they so recently left. They are aware, as they have not had time to shut out their spirituality, as that is what happens to so many children on the earth plane.*

*Without guidance a child loses his spirituality very quickly and begins to reach for worldly ways. The little ones that pass over are surrounded in spirit with much love and light. They usually 'grow up in spirit' and become very strong powerful guides because of their level of purity. Very few of these 'little ones' return to earth because being the pure spiritual souls that they are, they do not need to learn all the karmic lessons.*

*So therefore the lesson is usually for those left behind, and believe me, their lives will have been touched by these souls. It does seem like a harsh and cruel lesson but remember each soul is on this earth plane through choice and in order to enrich his spiritual path. So each man has his own destiny, his own path to follow.*

*I know that you are eager to learn more and may feel that these lessons are a simplified version of what you already know, but there is a purpose and plan to everything. You know that the spiritual path demands a lot of patience and acceptance. Nothing can be rushed. To everything, there IS A SEASON AND A REASON.*

*The 'girls' spend a lot of time in the Spiritual Nursery. They are drawn to the baby souls and make them laugh with all their play-acting for them. Darling one, you do so much with them when you travel into the astral, you feel their frustrations, but also sense their joy, their wonderful uniting and love. Don't let them be forgotten. Why are people ignoring what happened to them and yet it continues to happen? It is time that publicity is needed again, not to open old wounds or cause any unnecessary heartache, but the girls say it is needed again. 'Lest they forget', to find the needle in a haystack, one must keep looking. There can be nothing more important than that.*

*I must leave you now, but a personal message before I go.*

*In previous writing I have said that I tell everyone Pam will question everything and turn it inside out and back to front, but don't change what I tell you or Beverly! I know that my spelling goes off as I am doing great speeds when writing. Could write reams and reams to you! Don't be sad, it hurts me so much. I am always at your side.*

*Love, love and love you, yours eternally,*

*Raymond*

## ***SIXTH LESSON***

*My dearest beloved,*

*Oh I do so love and adore you and it is so difficult at times to have to sit back and watch you endure so much pain. Not one thing happens without a reason and causing a chain of events to happen. You are well protected and greatly loved by the spiritual realm.*

*Only by continuing your current path and purpose are we allowed to remain together through eternity. We don't lose our personalities when we move to spirit; it is merely a shift of consciousness. If we didn't like doing a thing in our earthly existence we don't like doing it in spirit either.*

*That is why I am so thankful for the computer! Bert likes to relay messages, rather than have to communicate himself. He sends Yvonne all his love and blessings and wants her to know that he wished he knew as much about life as he knows now, especially while he was living it.*

*So I have to commence our lesson:*

*** *You often visit our world. This is done by means of astral travel. This is when the soul separates from the earth body and travels into our realms. Most people do this form of travel but are not aware of it. But they often wake up with what they feel has been very real and strange dreams.*

*Spirit uses this means of contact as soul development. There are many reasons as to why you would travel into the astral, one of the most important being for a renewal of energy. As it has been explained, we work on vibration levels and it requires a tremendous amount of energy to enable us to come through to do our work.*

*So the person we use as a vessel does require their energy to constantly be restored and built up. The person we use would travel into astral and be taken to the place of healing. There the purest thoughts and vibration levels recharge their energy and allow us to continue to use them as vessels. People who are ill are often taken into spirit to the astral and if it is not their time to leave the earth plane, they receive healing and guidance. We also have the need for astral travelers, to help with our rescue work.*

*Often when one passes over into our realms they are not prepared, as it is a swift passing. They are at a loss and confused and in their current state, can only relate to other human forms. Therefore the earthly soul, who is now being used in the rescue work, would have to explain to the lost soul that he has entered another realm and level of consciousness, creating an acceptance around him and slowly guiding him towards the light of the spiritual realm.*

*They are then able to go with the spirit guides, first to the place of healing, followed by the place of learning, where they gain my insight and understanding of the light. The astral too, can be a meeting place for two human souls. One living far away is able to meet with you in astral. It's a place where you gain much knowledge and understanding, a place of contemplation*

*Astral Travel is a gift to be attained; it cannot be forced but is achieved through relaxation and with the help of your spirit guides. Although your guide travels with you and offers a form of protection, you have to travel through several levels of attainment.*

*There are many lost and mischievous souls on the lower levels, so it is important that before you go to sleep at night, you do ask for protection and guidance! On the start of your astral travel you are taken to an entrance gate where you receive a blessing and are cleansed of your earthly vibrations. You are dressed in a spiritual robe, leaving your garments behind.*

*The soul traveler is connected to his earthly body with a silver cord, much like the umbilical cord at birth. This ensures his safe return. So let this lesson be blessed.*

*Love, love and love you for eternity,*

*Raymond*

## *Seventh Lesson*

*My Dearest Beloved One,*

*Although we are in communication daily I do know how you wait for these communications, and as you have seen by now, they are merely confirmations of all we have already shown you. I miss you so much at times. I am always beside you but our paths were always running together. I can help you so much more and we must believe in the universal laws and principals. There is higher reasoning than ours.*

*You do have a higher purpose to serve and it is slowly being revealed to you so that you may understand it in full. There are many rewards awaiting you, you have come through all the trials and tests. You will be called upon soon to help a friend who will suffer the loss of her husband but you will be able to guide her through it.*

*Heather will have a health problem that will cause you to worry, but the outcome will be good. Your spiritual abilities are becoming stronger so do not be afraid, for we are doing a lot of development work on you and moving events very fast. This would not normally be possible except for the link that you and I have between each other. I have to go to the lesson for the day so Dearest One, I continue with the universal light of love, understanding and protection.*

*** *We live in a world beyond human understanding. We have no 'matter,' rather everything around us is made up of our thoughts. We too, are rewarded by the lives we have lived on the earth plane. There are different levels of attainment and one may progress at will. We wear robes symbolizing our level of attainment.*

*Upon transition, the robe that you wear would be white until you are ready to move onto spiritual attainment. This cycle of soul development only takes place on the seventh plane, the plane of contentment and fulfillment and growth. As you progress, so the colour of your robe changes. This is so that others are aware of your level of soul growth and you also work on the colour vibrations of your progress.*

*The colour of the new learner would be green, and then progress through to blue and a whole spectrum of colour until finally he reaches the highest level, which is violet. It is not easy to attain this knowledge, some would rather stay in their newfound levels of peace and contentment, but eventually some form of movement is required. Even in our world change and progress is inevitable.*

*The lessons taught are many. We are taught to become guides to those who are still on the earth plane. This gift is not easily given and once given it is a hard task, for we may not interfere with any cosmic laws or principles and the karmic lessons of the earth.*

*We live and operate on different levels and there are seven planes and seven principles, which govern us. Each plane has its own level of vibrations rising from the negative of the first plane to the pure positive elements of the seventh plane.*

*Often when you have dreadful nightmares or see ugly images, it is the poor souls on the first level who linger on the earth plane vibrations, who refuse to move on. Negativity begets negativity, so these are usually the souls who were evil on the earth plane and are totally unrepentant of their deeds and so have not risen above the negativity in their souls. There is no hell and damnation, they are free to move onto soul progression any time they wish.*

*It is negativity that is self- imposed. Transition can be very traumatic for those who have no spiritual knowledge. We wish for people to know they have nothing to fear. It is the uncertainty of the unknown that they fear. Nature is a law unto us all.*

*Life is merely a way to our final destination. Spiritual people gladly embrace death. They are greeted by guides and able to go straight to the place of learning where they receive their higher colours.*

*They are, through knowledge able to reach higher levels and become guides themselves. Others choose to return to the earth plane to continue their lesson there. There is nothing to fear! Everyone is involved in a God plan. Only those who are materialistic and so wish to cling to the earth plane to continue their lessons there become aimless and wandering. They should spend more time enriching their souls, which they can carry into the next world.*

*Our world is beautiful. It cannot be described in your earth words, you cannot be made to grasp or understand the physics involved, for although there is no 'matter' we do have beautiful buildings and structures. I am constantly in awe of them and have sat in on many planning developments, utterly amazing and mind-blowing stuff. Had I such knowledge on the earthly realm?? I love the even flow and endless possibilities of these structures. Before I linger too long on my own interest in these buildings I must continue with the lesson.*

****Transition is so wonderful. A miracle, a movement of nature, as in birth, so in death. We should weep at births and laugh and be happy at deaths. How strange the world that it has such distorted views - Happy when one moves into an imperfect lower vibration of the earth and sad when one has reached the goals and learned the lessons and can now go home! Death is a graduation! If a person passes over after a long illness or simply believes he is going to sleep forever, he will first be taken to the place of healing.*

*This is a huge and very beautiful building that glows within a great healing light. Here he is given much tender loving care and his spirit is 'built up' and ready to move on. It can take hours or years measured by your time. Death is not actually felt, it is easier to "die" than it is to be born. At the moment of death or impact, as with the bullet entering my body, the soul escapes any bodily pain. As one stands watching from a distance as an observer, one is enveloped into a great white light of peace and great love, a feeling of well - being, never experienced before, and it is so easy.*

*The only difficulty is to leave loved ones behind, as you wish for them to share this wonderful experience with you and long to reassure them that you are better than all right! They cry tears for you and should not, for you are weeping for them having to live out their karma. End of lesson for today.*

*Love, love and love you, yours eternally,*

*Raymond*

## *EIGHTH LESSON*

*Dearest One and most beloved,*

*I want to give you all the re-assurance that you are never alone and to tell you to remember that all 'your' greatest efforts and successes have been born of your sheer frustration. I am with you always and I watch the wonderful progress you have made with me in spirit.*

*As I grow and develop you share my knowledge, so we will always share a special bond. You are and will always be my soul mate! You are going to be very busy and there is a lot of development taking place. There is not much to give you at present. You know I do watch over everyone.*

*I do so love, love and love you.*

*Raymond*

*The lesson begins today begins with Karma:*

**** Karma is all about the laws of give and take. Literally meaning, AS YOU SOW SO SHALL YOU REAP. The meaning of the word karma is Action! Each is responsible for his own Action! If you plant seeds of love, happiness and service, you will reap the same action. Not only do we shape our own karma by action, but also by thoughts.*

*Like attracts like, so too negative thoughts will draw negativity towards you. But positive thoughts will attract positive energy. All around you, the human body and the whole universe is made up of energy and matter, your thoughts are very much part of this energy field and part of you.*

*You all live out three different types of karma, the first karma is what we have stored from our past lives and past actions; the lessons we have to currently learn through our present lives; and the payments we have to make, they have to be paid back in full. So the second karma we live out is repaying our karmic debts and duties, this we do both consciously and unconsciously. We live through both pain and joy! Gain and losses! The second karma gives you a challenge to do 'good'. To always react with love, kindness and forgiveness!*

*By returning a hurt inflicted upon you, you are merely bringing the same pain to yourself time and time again. It's difficult, but bless the situation as a karmic debt repaid and move on. The third karmic cycle you are living is very important because by your present actions you are building up karma for the future re-incarnations and your very actions now are shaping future karmic debts and relationships. So the most important lesson to learn is the law of karma. If you hurt another, even by accident, you are hurting yourself. If you lie to another, you are lying to yourself. And so, Karma and the other three cycles of it run side by side the one merging into the other. Our past affects our present, our present affects our future. There are no mistakes in the universe! And so I leave this lesson with a blessing.*

*Love you and give you lots of protection and power. You do a lot of astral work with me and you're amazing, so proud of you!*

*Eternally yours,*

*Raymond*

## *NINTH LESSON*

*My Dearest Beloved,*

*Never doubt that you are given spiritual guidance in all that you do, it's so easy to question why, but each step and each day is taking you to a higher purpose and a higher level of attainment. You have achieved all you need to in physical growth and are being led along to achieve spiritual growth and with it achievement and direction. There is a purpose to every event that is happening, let it be okay that the universe is guiding your path and have acceptance of that.*

*Heather will be able to see new direction in about 8 weeks and there are going to be major changes taking place all around her. But it will be progressive and put an end to the restrictions and uncertainty that they have been feeling.*

*Norm has many positive developments occurring and a fast moving element that brings in a lot of new opportunities. Listen to that gut feeling!*

*Lesson begins:*

**** Marriage is in harmony with God, it is the perfect blending of two souls. The ultimate desires we bring to the earth plane is the desire of a union with our soul mates, the joining of two souls who have joined together in many incarnations. This one soul is your sanctuary. The joy and blessings of your soul mates has no bounds or barriers, it can have bonds or connections that last long after the physical or earthly bonds are broken.*

*Soul mates are spirit links, which bind together for all eternity. A soul connection is what we are destined for and meant to experience, but in the fast moving and physical world it is a sad fact that many, many souls do not meet up with their soul mates.*

*Lust is one where the physical feelings lead or rather misleads one into a relationship of strong desire. These physical urges are strong enough to unite two beings yet often end up in deception, hate, hurt and unhappiness. Seldom does a relationship based on the physical alone bring any joy, but rather heartache.*

*Man has also become so rational that often he cannot proceed beyond that level. So! Like attracts like! in the universal law of give and take. While living in an unhappy marriage or partnership one cannot grow spiritually as it is detrimental to ones psychic growth. One soul traps the other and the cycle continues. It's good to realize when the time comes to move on.*

*When the lesson has been learned the soul growth has occurred, there is new energy and new lessons to learn. Don't stay stuck in one cycle. Soul mates is the linking of two souls, bound to each other through eternity, a union based on the spiritual, physical and mental energies, the finding of yourself within another, and by doing so, receiving the universes blessings. A noble and higher level of love, that is forever binding and brings in true happiness that remains within the soul pattern for eternity.*

*And so blessed be this lesson.*

*My dearest Pamie, you and I are fine examples of the lesson. Remember the universal link, even though you are still a very much physical and earthly being, you have a stronger link to the spirit world than most, and that is because your soul mate is in spirit and it was meant to be this way.*

*You will know why you are going to have a relationship in your life. You were never meant to be alone but you will have to settle for far less than anything we experienced, that is our soul connection. Now you will have a companion to ease the burdens and your aloneness. Just continue to have patience and acceptance, all will come to you, all will be provided, have faith, you only need to look at Raybert to know we will provide for you always.*

*Bert is working hard at directing you to all the people and energy you need to progress with the plan. He is determined that the conference center be done. He says to tell Yvonne he was laughing at her putting on her shoes this morning and she has been so distracted lately that he has been moving things around in order for her to think, she will know what he means. He is always around uplifting her and trying to get her to laugh. He blesses you for all you do for his family.*

*I love, love and love you for eternity,*
*Raymond*

Yvonne had told me that she was just about to leave for work when fortunately she noticed she was wearing one navy shoe and one black one. She also tripped over her shoes, as they were not lying in the usual place. She was so amused at Bert's message.

Heather, my sister, who had been extremely ill in Zambia, as Ray had mentioned in one of his previous writings, had contracted Malaria, and subsequently suffered a stroke. I e-mailed the writing to them, unbeknown to me at the time, that she was already seriously ill in hospital. Neil, her husband, was able to take her this message from Ray, which was encouraging to them both. She later told me that she had suffered a near death experience and since then has felt Ray's presence often.

My mother who was 87 years old at the time lived with them and had been seriously ill with malaria. She too suffered had a mild stroke and had fallen and broken her pelvic bone. I immediately placed her on distant healing and the results were astounding. Although we expected her to be in hospital for at least six weeks, within days, she was her sprightly old self, back home walking with a walking frame. It was comforting to know that they were both being taken care of.

Norman had progressed in his business and was encouraged by Ray's messages and continual guidance. When I first told him about the communication that I was receiving he was very skeptical. His beliefs now are so strong as more and more proof of his brother's guidance and predictions had become a reality.

## *TENTH LESSON*

*Dearest Pam, Beloved One,*

*I have been away, restoring my spiritual growth and energy. We too need to rebuild our strength from time to time even though it is easier for us as we have seen the divine plan.*

*In order for us to assist the enlightened souls such as your self, we do pass through negative energy fields in order to reach all. So we too need to replace energy. But even when you do not get the writings from me which we give for your need and encouragement, you still receive spiritual education and growth while your body is resting.*

*This is when you are in touch with your inner levels of perception and gain much of the highest and truest impressions that come to you in the early morning hours. You must trust yourself fully to the Universe and the Universe will never fail you. You are an interpreter of the Universal truths for others and are blessed.*

*Blessed too be the lesson that follows:*

**** To be at one with God and the Universe is to be at peace. Once you come to this higher realization you will never have fear and always a sense of protection. Become conscious of the Universal principals to work for the good of all mankind, in a spirit of harmony and peace and acceptance of each one's level of soul development.*

*Things that cause sorrow pain or bereavement should not cause pain! By following the Universal path you will clearly see things in their right places and gain insight into all things as you know and understand their place in the Universal plan of things. The things you open yourself up to will always come to be in the negative or positive, so each must know themselves and their powers, and use their Universal links wisely.*

*Don't say, "It comes to you!" "You can't help it!" It's all about attitude of mind, 'like attracts like', both negative and positive. If you display faith in the Universe and use individual power for the good of all, you will reap great benefits. Always be true to yourself and never surrender your own individuality, which is part of each one's personal power. Customs, connections and restrictions have stopped others from spiritual growth and individuality. If you surrender your individuality you merely become a slave to conventions, no growth, always trying to please others. Preserve your individuality and you become master. As you open yourself up more and more to the Universal laws and principals you allow it's energy to pour through you and in that find the peace and power you need.*

*One's who have reached this great level of attainment are the spiritual people who are individual, not belonging to one creed or group, rather working as 'individuals'. They are the ones who give out blessings and comfort, the one's who, just by their presence can give hope and encouragement, change sorrow into joy, fear into courage, despair into hope and fear or weakness, into courage and power. They radiate calm and spirituality because they have found the core, the center of all things, the Universal energy and laws, the spiritual vibrations, which are not always clearly visible in everyday living.*

*Blessings.*

*Dearest One, most Beloved, just to re-assure you that I am with you everyday in every way, never doubt that for one moment. My spiritual growth is your growth too.*

*As always, love, love and love you,*

*Raymond*

## *ELEVENTH LESSON*

*Darling Pamie and most beloved,*

*I do hear the questions! But I can't always give the answers. They are available to you, simply keep your mind and heart open to the divine flow, realize that even now, we have a oneness of spirit and soul and always carry that realization within you. Do not concern yourself with practical matters.*

*They are taken care of, you will never be at a loss for anything, you can be free of cares, knowing that higher powers are indeed guiding you and free you of practical responsibilities. Uncertainties can only come because you sometimes row against the tide, know that whatever your doubts and uncertainties are, you are working towards a divine plan and we work together in oneness of the soul. Yes there are many healers! But your job is to heal the mind, which in turn will heal the body.*

*The lesson begins:*

**** Each morning is a fresh beginning! A new start! All yesterdays should be yesterdays and all tomorrows should be tomorrows, for how we live this day will shape our tomorrows, and even our future destiny and karmic debts. It is sufficient then to know that the way we live today determines our tomorrows. This knowledge, if lived and practiced by all, will bring each person in touch with their higher self, and bring out all of ones positive qualities.*

*There are many who call themselves 'teachers' or 'mentors', yet they rob others of their free will. They enjoy the power and control they have over the fate and destiny of others. Look closely to see their personal motives and personal gains. He, who claims to have all the truth and the only truth, knows so little. He causes much damage.*

*The true teacher is one who is able to give true knowledge, and awaken the individual to his own intuitive sources so that he may become his own interpreter and have free will and personal direction over his own life. Each soul progresses through his own lessons and self-knowledge.*

*One must be willing to trust him self fully to the universe and the principals. Hold onto the beliefs of oneness with the universe. It has to be complete trust. Half hearted trust brings uncertainty. Total trust brings rewards. Simply do today what gets offered to you, always using the principals of divine love for the good of all. Today's supplies will be granted to you and based on what you do today, tomorrow's supplies in spiritual and physical life will be granted to you. See how simple the principal laws of the Universe are? So ends our brief lesson.*

*We are so proud of all your efforts, never doubt you are working towards a divine plan. It's not easy because you cannot see the results but it's very important.*

*Love, love and love you in eternity.*

*Raymond*

## *TWELFTH LESSON*

*Darling One,*

*How I love you and share your sense of aloneness, it will not always be so, but for now you have so much to accomplish and will continue to do so. You are right to feel that an important event is about to occur, proving to you, that all your efforts have not been in vain. You have received a blessing. I would prefer to be at the computer but time and energy is short, so I have to write while the opportunity presents itself, I love, love and do love you.*

**** 'Fear' and 'worry' block our spiritual development and growth. It corrodes and tears down the body's organism too! It has a weakening and tearing down effect on both body and mind and does little for soul growth. With it, brings anger, jealousy, faultfinding, and all the negative traits that bring corroding tearing down effects. Negativity breeds negativity. Whatever mood you set in your mind, your soul and the universal energies respond to.*

*The law of attraction is based on Universal principals. Our thoughts attract and much can be accomplished through them, but allow doubt or fear to enter and you neutralize a tremendous power. The power of every life is therefore based on our thought patterns. It is the Universal Principal. Out mutual thoughts determine the quality of our lives. Every thought has value to the soul. A strong positive mind will attract strong, positive elements in all things. It will also be of value to others as it uplifts them.*

*A weak and negative mind draws negative elements and responses. It also becomes a burden to others as it pulls them down too. The human body does have limitations, not so the mind. Bring your lives into universal harmony by adopting positive thought cycles. Always be conscious to the power of this energy that links one to the Universal Forces. By doing this we can keep in mind that the Universal laws and principals are in continues operation, whether or not we are conscious of them, we are continually attracting forces and conditions that are linked to our own thoughts. If we fail in our thoughts, we fail in everything. And so my love ends this lesson.*

*There are going to be some major developments with the 'girls'. You are going to receive some very important information about them shortly. Never doubt for one moment, the information you are given.*

*Love, love and love you for all eternity,*

*Raymond*

## *THIRTEENTH LESSON*

*Darling One, Most beloved Pamie,*

*What a wonderful path we have traveled these past years. Thank you for sharing your soul development with me. It is a hard path ...*

****Life is a soul teacher; it allows soul growth and development. The harder the lesson the greater the aura of soul growth and development. Each day the Universe provides perfect opportunities for soul growth. We all need to be more perceptive of the opportunities, everyone is born psychic and in tune with the wisdom of the universe, but this is blocked almost at birth, by traditions and built in barriers of the families we are born into.*

*But psychic impressions remain with us throughout our lives and they are always there in various forms. They may come as a hunch, a vague sense of feeling something about to happen, or a quick or unexplained flash of insight into a problem or situation. Visions may come to the most logical analytical mind through dreams, for the subconscious mind will lead the conscious mind. It can sometimes come to you in thoughts, just a passing thought or the feeling that you receive outside communication or thought within your own head.*

*How often have you heard the phrase 'it just popped into my head' or 'where did that come from'? It can manifest itself in smell i.e. you catch a fragrance, or a whiff in the air that reminds you of someone or something important. Most people, because they work on the logical and analytical mind, and do not use the subconscious, go through life unaware of the powerful expressions of the subconscious mind that is at work all the time, giving constant guidance and direction.*

*Psychic impressions are felt through live senses and do not need a lot of practice to learn, just 'acceptance' and to learn to listen to our bodies. The human body is like a sensor, as it constantly gives out and absorbs energy around it.*

*The subconscious mind monitors this and gives it all to the conscious mind. All we have to do is listen, slow down our busy lives and <u>KNOW</u> that we* *have all the answers. Nothing is accidental in the Universe, LISTEN TO YOUR BODY !! It's not hard to do.*

*Dearest One, my passing, was not an ending, but just a beginning for both you and me. One day you will understand why it had to be so.*

*Love, love and love you eternally,*

*Raymond*

### *FOURTEENTH LESSON*

First Beverley's guide came through!

*Greetings, many blessings light and love. Beverley we have explained to you how we work on vibration levels. We are constantly shifting and changing to higher vibration levels and it does take some time for you to get in tune with the higher vibration. It's during this 'tuning phase' that you feel that you have lost contact with your guides or have lost your gift of writing. This is never so.*

*You have us with you always, it's just your vibration levels which are being adjusted, and while this is happening, you are receiving healing and cleansing. Your energy level too has to be raised to meet the vibration level. There is much going on but we are always there to guide and assist you. Just have acceptance that things do move a lot slower in the Spirit World. We do not measure the time as mankind does. What a failing that is, for time cannot be measured. Have you noticed how one hour seems a lifetime when things are bad, and yet an hour flies by as if a minute when things are good?*

*NO! Time cannot be measured, so have patience and acceptance. There is a reason for everything and you will find greater spiritual progress. The spiritual path is a difficult one for you, as you will continuously have tests of your faith. You accepted the path of your karma. There are no mistakes in the Universe, In love and light.*

*Lessons will proceed:*

*Greetings my eternal love Pamie,*

*As was written to Beverley, there is a great adjustment taking place in vibration levels. You will feel disassociated, different, because you exist on a different vibration level to others, but knowing this, learn to have patience with them. It's not always possible to communicate at will and those who do have no real power and knowledge. You too, are continuously tested. Remember you have a higher purpose and you do have to be pure in soul, no matter how 'silent' and 'alone' you may feel. You have never given up spiritually.*

*We cannot give you advice all the time. You have to learn your own lesson, as it is your soul growth. Tell Donald there will be the progression he wants, but that the month of October is a more favorable time for it. Reg is here too now and he wants to say Hello...... That's all, just Hello! Heinrich is in financial problems and there is going to be some new development into his past errors. He is in a panic but the laws of karma are at work there. Bert has been making tremendous progress, he says he has been working full time to get Yvonne to laugh, but she has been irritated by his tricks, so he says, " Sorry!"*

*He laughed when he said, "Who did she give his shoes to?" He is laughing and says, "A man only need walk a mile in his shoes". Bert always gets us to laugh in the most serious moments. He wants people to know he did MAKE IT UP and although he does not have his "angel wings" he is there. I have to send him on his way so that we can get down to some writing. Before I do so I want to say that I am so proud of you. I tell them here, "She will do what she will do. She will be what she will be!" You amaze them not me! I know you. "That's my Pamie!"*

*** *Those who embrace the spiritual path are the true children of light. By taking on the hard task, and often unrewarding task of being of service to your fellow man, you tune into divine Universal light, that everyone does have within them, but not many are able to allow the light to shine forth freely and into the lives of others. It is good to acknowledge the 'Inner Light' that has been entrusted to you, everyday. Tune yourself into the Universe and awaken and acknowledge your Inner Light.*

*Imagine yourself switching on the light, feeling the warmth of it within you, and giving you a feeling of warmth divine love and energy. Accept that you are a pure channel for this light; imagine the light going from you and lighting everyone it touches.*

*When God said, "Let there be light!" Our existence began. The world will be a brighter and more loving place if each person could share his/her light with another. By sending your light out each day you do make the world a brighter place and attract all those in need of help and assistance. Those in the dark area are drawn towards your light.*

*Although there is a calling and a need for the children of the light to assist others, they must also keep in mind that their first duty is towards themselves.*

*They must never doubt that progress is being made and that as the light shines out to direct the lives of others, so too will it lead them towards their advancement. There will always be a challenge and tests along the way. That is the lesson of life. But as long as you allow your inner light to guide you, you move forward in LOVE, LIGHT and PROTECTION. So ends the lesson.*

*I do so love, love and love you.*

*Eternally yours,*

*Raymond*

Bev called me a few hours later; she had felt Ray's presence and could sense that he was very irritated,

Herewith:

*'You and Pam have the answers before you all the time, but you don't look with your eyes.*

*Do you want the answer to 'Soul'? Yes?*

***S***=*SPIRITUAL*

***O***=*ONENESS!*

***U***=*UNIVERSAL!*

***L***= *LOVE!*

## *FIFTEENTH LESSON*

*Dearest Pamie,*

*I do so adore you. How you cope with the mountains of work we send you I have no idea? But I never doubt your ability to see anything through.*

*We have been very busy and as you rightly know, we do go quietly just before and during the passing of a number of souls, as we are needed to guide them over. Yes, I have been touching you ever so lightly while you sleep. Sorry I didn't mean to wake you! But it's just that sleeping like that, you look so vulnerable and alone and I need to let you know that you are never alone! I am beside you, helping you and guiding you. We've always made a great team.*

*Our lesson for the day follows, may it be blessed:*

*** *The Universe is made up of light, colour and vibration. Those who are guided by us have the awareness of this light of Christ consciousness. It helps them to remain focused and they can move along with the constant changing vibrations of light and colour that guides them into positive constructive channels.*

*Everything living has an aura of magnetic power and light, an energy source radiating from it. This is not always visible to the untrained eye, but an aura reveals a great deal. Since there is no death in any form, one merely passes to another vibration level and begins living in another sphere or wavelength, and life continues in a perfectly natural way in spirit bodies.*

*We want you to love all animals, because they too are part of the Universe and also exist in spirit. In death it's only a physical sheath that has been discarded. The soul lives on. Most people only seek 'spiritual' help when the going gets tough! They expect 'spirit' to have all the answers. We long to help, but we may only work on 'their' understanding and 'own' realities. It's very difficult for us, working on the vibrations of light, colour and love, to open up even a tiny part of the mind that has been shut off and had it's growth stifled, even harder to get a ray of light to shine in.*

*What most people do not realize is that transformation of any kind requires a great deal of courage. Yes! "Ask and you shall receive," but almost all the answers are available within ones self and one needs to be in tune with ones own inner light. Any progress in life comes through evolution, it does not happen overnight, yet the light is always above one and all. Often one may feel untouched by it and yet the contact is always there, as are the answers. Once you are aware of the light in your life, the Universal principal applies. Light received needs to be light shared, so that it forms a chain reaction of light and love that will illuminate the world. So ends our lesson.*

*May the light continue to guide and direct you as you draw others into the powerful vibrations of love and light.*

*Love, love and love you,*

*Eternally yours,*

*Raymond.*

## *SIXTEENTH LESSON*

*Dearest One,*

*There is not much energy today so we must move on to the lesson. Know that I am with you at all times. In all ways, be assured that your strength and courage will never falter.*

*The lesson begins:*

**** Intuition is not a rare gift or something that is only found in gifted people, everyone has intuition and everyone has the ability to develop this natural part of self. Yet like any natural gift or talent it needs to be nurtured or practiced at, it needs to be developed like any other function of the human body. Many people wonder at how intuitive impressions differ from the objective consciousness.*

*The first thing is that intuitive impressions come from the vibration levels of love and understanding. They are more tolerant and non- judgmental. They are in harmony with the cosmic and Universal laws and principals, whereas objective consciousness limits our thinking and is based on 'self preservation'. It's a decision making factor that often stifles intuition. Where objective consciousness is about the self, our own needs, egos and gratification, the intuition is all about the unity of mankind and their connection to the Soul and God.*

*Because of the thinking mind it is easy to deceive oneself into hearing intuitive answers, but those that one wants to hear, rather than allowing the true flow of intuition! Following surface feelings, rather than getting the real answers from deep within. Intuition gives guidance and direction from the deep, within ones soul consciousness. Everyone has all the answers available deep within themselves.*

*We are always directed and guided by them. This may come in the form of a hunch i.e. these arrive in higher thought patterns or feelings, and always come with a feeling of upliftment and light, an element of surprise, or a feeling of "YES, that's the answer! Why didn't I think of that before?" It's a sense of thought combined with uplifting feelings. Sometimes intuition comes through a mental picture as in a dream or meditation, or even just arrives by going to certain places at a certain time.*

*Do not ever be discouraged by a feeling of getting no response or answer when seeking an answer, the UNIVERSE KNOWS AND DOES ANSWER ALL YOUR QUESTIONS. You might not receive an answer in a blinding flash of revelation, but you can be assured that, as you ask, EVENTS ARE TAKING PLACE TO PROVIDE YOU WITH THE RIGHT ANSWERS AT THE RIGHT TIME, and that you will receive a sign that your questions are being answered, even if you don't understand the answer all at once. You can be assured that you will! - 'Ask and you shall receive'. So continue to apply your effort in love and light. May this lesson be blessed!*

*Love, love and love you eternally,*

*Raymond*

CONTINUATION OF LESSON 16

*Dearest One and most Beloved,*

*Today there is a buzz because it's Pamie's birthday! and you are sent many blessings. You are blessed and loved today and always. How mankind measures in time!! When everything is Universal, and you my love, and I, are eternal.*

*Today you have been granted many spiritual gifts to add to those you already have. You've earned them well beloved, congratulations! Remember the birthday surprise you gave me? Well today I can surprise you. Can you feel the buzz? You have reached the cycle of purification and completion. Many new exciting developments are about to take place. The last lesson was incomplete, because of the low energy we only did part of it.*

*So the lesson continues:*

****All beings, every creature, every plant, everything has a source of light. All levels of intelligence, whether they those of highest rank, or those of lowest rank, are connected to that one source of divine light originating from God. They form a long line, so that the higher rank shed their light on* *the lower rank. So, all beings originate from the one source of light, all parts are part of the Universal WHOLE.*

*Therefore every being has the potentiality of Spiritual Awareness and Power. Wealth, power, everything is within the self, and not in physical things created around the self. In times of trouble and uncertainty you only have to turn inward to the light within yourself to receive all the divine answers, and inspiration.*

*If only one was aware that all tomorrows are created by the actions of today, what a better place the world would be. The Universal principal here is that tomorrow is taken care of by the actions of today. Every living being needs to know and understand that they are a channel for this Universal light, the source which comes from God, and is unlimited. The attitude that you are better than anyone else or having judgmental views limits your spiritual growth.*

*Know that the divine light is always working within you to bring a divine plan into action, that of love and harmony for all. Knowing that! will always bring peace in storms and direction in times of darkness. May this lesson be blessed.*

*Love, love and love you.*

*Eternally yours for all time.*

*Raymond*

Bev had been going through a difficult time when this lesson was channeled through to her, hence the lack of energy. After she had taken down the lesson, the automatic writing continued with the following message for her:

*You always give advice but rarely take it, so we are not going to tell you what to do, but just give to you some things to think carefully on! You are spirit in a body, not a body in a spirit. The Master works to a divine plan. Nothing is ever done without a reason. You have self-will, but it must be controlled. Faith and positive thinking are essential to your development. Overcoming Karma must be endured. Love yourself! We love you! Let the*

*Universal love shine through your hurt. As you give, you are assured you will receive. You're in too much hurry and always stubbornly wanting to do things in your way.*

*Acknowledge the light that protects and guides you. Try to stay on the road and not rush off to pick a flower on the side - It looks pretty, but soon dies. Enough to think on! We love you and surround you with a healing light of love and protection. Look around you and see those who do love and value you, those who give you strength and purpose too.*

*Blessings,*

*Raymond*

## *SEVENTEENTH LESSON*

*My Dearest Pamie,*

*How glad I am for the joy of being able to work alongside you every moment. So much is happening in the spiritual realms at the moment. There is going to be a wave of new consciousness and that is what you have to prepare others for. Not to rely so much on the tomorrows and what may happen or is yet to be, but rather to realize that today is so important, for what you do today, is what your tomorrow will be based on.*

*The principals of the Universe apply AS YOU SOW, SO SHALL YOU REAP. With that knowledge each person is capable of shaping their own future in the way they wish it to go. Today is called the "Present" because that is what it is, a present given to you by the Universe, and tomorrow, another 'gift' will be given to you, a 'present'!*

*Your vibration levels are increasing and you could find yourself feeling more tired. It is important that you lie down for about an hour every afternoon and have your quiet 'tuning time', that way you restore your energy.*

*Everything is working out for you and the answers are within yourself as follows today's lesson:*

****You may wonder how we are able to give these lessons, as discussed in earlier lessons. Everyone has intuition!! 'Intuition', comes from the Latin word 'Intuare', which means 'Teacher!'*

*Everyone has all the answers within ones self through this inner teacher. Once you realize this source and can connect to it, the 'God Force' is easily able to enter your life and give you the information and guidance you seek. This is often called 'channeling' and the advice can be given to you through thought patterns, speech or writing, as we are using for these lessons.*

*While in a state of channeling, the person being channeled will disconnect from their own self and personality, their minds become free enough to allow a spiritual consciousness to link telepathically with energy, vibration and frequency levels. This is always done with the knowledge and the free will of one being channeled, free to disconnect the link at any time.*

*No one is ever 'taken over' and free will is never violated. A psychic then becomes like a spiritual phone, a link and connection between one dimension and another. The spiritual and cosmic laws apply and therefore guides cannot interfere unless asked to help. Then only can guidance be given! Free will and karma cannot be interfered with or changed.*

*We cannot give impossible answers or magic solutions, as is often expected. Each individual has come to the earth plane to learn certain lessons and that is how they experience soul growth, the answers lie within each one...The intuition.... The teacher! Every living thing, all spirit, is energy, vibrating at a certain frequency.*

*God is the center of all the energy, vibrating at the highest level and the source of all other energy. Every living thing is interlinked to this continuous flow of divine energy through all parts of the whole. When one becomes aware of the energy and vibration levels that exist within one and around one, then one is able to tap into the conscious level of it and attain communication with spiritual beings.*

*The very act of believing and accepting this leads already to an altered state of vibration or consciousness. If you do not tune into the right frequency on a radio, you will not hear the radio station that you want, so too is the way 'Spirit' communicate with psychics. May this lesson be blessed.*

*I love, love and love you.*

*Raymond*

## *EIGHTEENTH LESSON*

*Darling One, Pamie*

*It's always a pleasure to be able to write you these notes, just to confirm that link between you and I, and how it survives even in different vibration levels.*

*When you feel exhausted, as you have been, you can rest assured it's just because you are working on a higher vibration to that of your earthly one, but we do protect you. It has always been so difficult to express feelings in writing but you always brought out the best in me and still do.*

*I could never move away from that powerful link we have. From the moment I saw you I felt that eternal bond that nothing can ever break. Do not worry about future events, know that everything is working out to a divine plan and that there will be a great deal of developments taking place for you. Greet my loved ones for me. I am often with them. Dan sends his regards.*

*The lesson begins:*

**** Each one has an inner guide, an inner voice of wisdom. It is not necessary to go into solitude or places of retreat in order to find it, for it is within one at all times. By acknowledging its existence in the first place, one reaches a level of Universal understanding and is then easily able to tap into this vast resource of knowledge. The inner guide is just oneself, unique to the self as an individual.*

*It knows all about ones life purpose, ones previous incarnations, and where one is being led in this current existence. Retreat or solitude is not the best way to get in touch with this inner knowledge, for the inner self, the inner knowledge and guidance are there to help the outer self learn lessons through life's experiences and relationships.*

*Even the trials, problems and temptations are given to one to experience soul growth and to make one aware of one's limitations and weaknesses, and for one to emerge a wiser and stronger person, more compassionate to the needs of one's fellowman.*

*One who has suffered through hardships attains a higher level of wisdom. This gives Universal knowledge and understanding and makes one able to use the inner guide to direct ones own life. Ones outer self, the image, the physical, is often very limited, but the inner self, the voice of wisdom, the psychic has no limitations. Everyone is born with the awareness of the inner self, the intuition, but as a child one is taught to ignore the psychic inner self and to develop the physical material outer self.*

*Because of that, an unbalanced development occurs and soon the use of the inner self is ignored and lost. Slowly the individual moves away from the spiritual pure being and relies solely on the physical self. Children still pure of this spiritual energy often talk of it and their parents label it as 'imagination', and so children learn only to accept that which is shown in realities.*

*Allowing these layers and veils of preconditioning to fall away and accepting the inner guidance that is within takes courage. It means letting go of the outer self, it means forgetting about what one looks like in the eyes of others and accepting simply what one IS. IT MEANS LETTING GO OF ANXIETY, FEAR ND WORRY AND ACCEPTING IN IT'S PLACE, TRUST, FAITH AND THE UNIVERSAL PRINCIPALS. ACCEPTANCE THAT ONES OWN INNER SELF, THE GOD GIVEN LIGHT WILL GUIDE US IN THE RIGHT DIRECTIONS.*

*Each incarnation teaches one further soul lessons and removes further layers until balance is achieved between the outer and inner self, that is then the experience of the true level of happiness that seems so evasive to so many. In order to seek knowledge and solutions, seek the knowledge of the higher self within.*

*There is no death, only a transition or transformation to a higher level of existence, as you always carry your soul within.*

*It therefore has all the answers. So ends the lesson, may it be blessed.*

*Love, love and love you eternally,*

*Raymond*

## *Nineteenth Lesson*

*Darling One, Pamie,*

*Raybert is a place of healing, it is a combination of your energy and mine, and it brings light to so many souls, both earthly and spiritual. There is so much growth around you and with you. Do not allow the petty issues of others to get you down, for just as I would have protected you on the earth plane, I still protect you in spirit.*

*If only the one that hurts you so, could see me standing right in front of his self righteous self, he would for one, be left speechless!*

*Don can expect a lot of surprises and upliftment for there is to be the growth he desires within the next five weeks.*

*Bert says Yvonne needs to make plans to include more, as there will be FIVE! He says he always gives her help and is also telling her to get someone to look at the problem in her washing machine. He sends love and light and lots of laughter to you all. He says, "If in doubt, just laugh".*

*My love, the lesson begins:*

****The purpose of these lessons is not so much as to describe life after transition, as the real vastness of our spiritual existence is way beyond the human mind that always seeks LOGIC, REASONING and SCIENTIFIC explanations. The colours, hues and vibrations are way beyond defining.*

*The lessons are meant to give guidance and help to people along their destined path, so that when their time comes, they are able to embrace the spiritual existence so much easier. Life as you know it, is a cycle, a term or AGREEMENT that you previously took on before your soul reincarnated to its current existence. YOU HAVE CHOSEN TO LIVE IT, and therefore must do so to the best of your ability and circumstances. Life is given to live and learn and so, it is important to accept and celebrate the passing through of each trial and tribulation, knowing it has lead to soul progression.*

*This way one reaches a new level of knowledge and understanding. If only each one could realize that they have made a pact to go through these lessons for soul progression, life would be so much more acceptable and easier. You do have to live your own life according to your own free will that the Universe has given you. You cannot expect or even want others to live it for you. You can seek advice or guidance but ultimately the decision does rest with you alone. Each person is daily making their own destinies by their actions and thoughts. Most seem to forget and ignore that life does carry on after death, and what you have left undone or unlearnt, will have to be done at some time.*

*If you leave the world without knowledge or growth, you do arrive in spirit that way. Being Spirit does not change you! You are your soul. That is the essence of you. If you learn lessons, use your life to gain knowledge and learn to love and be content, your soul arrives in spirit that way. Do not be mistaken or misled that you can live your life as you please and just arrive in the spiritual realm to a great welcome with love and forgiveness! For misdeeds, you simply just incur more karmic debts, which will need to be repaid.*

*It is never too late to be of service to others. Treat others, as you would like them to treat you. Steer clear of negativity, negative people and negative thoughts within yourself. Little things make huge soul progression. On the earthly plane you have a saying," It is God's Will". NO IT IS NOT! FOR IT IS YOUR WILL! Everything is incurred, debt and karma, which you have willingly taken on in order for the progression of your soul. What is destiny? Destiny is 'Yourself'! Let the light shine out with all the purity of the soul within. YOU ARE NEVER ALONE. Each person has a spiritual guide to help them carry the load of life. In our next lesson we will tell you about life guides. Until then Dear Ones, if you find yourself living in darkness, look inward for the shining light of your soul and allow it to embrace you and guide you in your lessons of life. May this lesson be blessed.*

*Love, love and love you in eternity,*

*Raymond*

Bert's message for Yvonne had her confused for a while. Yes the washing machine did need to be repaired but what could he possibly mean? *"Get ready for number five!"* She was appalled. Yes she would love to settle down again as she was very lonely, but five!

One of Yvonne's favorite sayings was, "As in no ways!!!" However two months after receiving this message she did meet a new man. He too had children. Although Yvonne had two of her own, her oldest daughter Melissa lived away from home, so she did in fact have to prepare her home for five people, including herself and her youngest daughter Marieta.

## *TWENTIETH LESSON*

*Dearest One Pamie,*

*I love, love, love you. You know about the line of energy running through Raybert property so never doubt the healing abilities. The water is continuously energized and re-energized and that is the colour blue that you see. Raybert will become known around the world for its powers of healing. Clearly you have been shown that Spirit is working with you towards a Universal plan.*

*Your efforts are about to bear rewards, we are so proud of you. Your faith and trust shall not be found wanting. We have been very busy preparing for a passing of souls again. It is sad that all the information that we passed on about the 'girls' is not being used for they are well onto their 'astral' paths and soul healing.*

*It is so difficult for us in spirit; we have to tune into the right vibration level before we can communicate and then we may not tamper with destiny or the soul path, but can only gently guide and give direction. It is very much like when you do a reading for someone. You can only give them direction and guidance, they retain their own free will and, you know the level of frustration when advice is given and not used, or when the clues subtly planted, have been ignored.*

*There is no need for me to guide my family members when they are on a roll.*

*Our lesson begins:*

**** Everyone has a soul guide or Guardian Angel. This is one you have been with in many past lives but who no longer needs to evolve on an earthly lesson and has completed their karma. These guides are connected to you from the moment of birth, to guide you and be of spiritual assistance to you. They are on the same vibration and use the same wave levels as you.*

*Very often they make themselves known and felt through your intuition and often help to shape 'coincidental' happenings and 'lucky breaks' in your life. Guides have evolved to a higher level due to their karmic debts repaid and it is still part of this debt that makes them want to guide others through life experiences. So often one feels alone, but no one is ever truly alone, your guides are right there giving you the purest of love and understanding.*

*They are God's messengers and their pure energy from the divine source of light gives guidance and direction. Often people will venture to a 'Guide Seeker' to be told, you have a Nun; you have an American Indian; you have a Japanese doctor; the imagination can stretch to the greatest levels, only you know within yourself who your life guide is. Sit in quiet meditation, welcome your guide into your heart and home, feel the warm glow of his/her radiant love surrounding you, enfolding you. A cloak of angel wings around you! A hug of divine powerful, Universal love! Talk to your Guardian as you would a friend, your guardian certainly knows more about you than any friend ever could. Sit in the silence and you will hear the name of your guide and it will unlock many doors for you.*

*Do keep in mind, that coming into contact with your guide by your total and acceptance and acknowledgement of the role they are playing in your life, will be a mind alerting event.*

*Because of the pure and divine energy it is often so moving an experience that it reduces one to tears. If you wish to 'see' your guide because of that human flaw of having to see, feel and touch, before having to believe; when all about you is energy, matter and vibration, but you need to see, sit in front of the mirror with only a candle alight, feel your guides love and devotion to you and ask that he may reveal himself to you.*

*Look into the mirror and gaze into your own face, slowly your features will change and take on the shape and form of your guardian angel, for he comes through you, to you. Your birth angel or guardian angel is the one who has taken on the task to guide and direct you through your lifetime on earth. In no way can your guide change your karma or direction, but he is always there, especially in times of crisis and need, and will help to ease the burdens.*

*Darling Pamie, at my funeral, I could smile, wave and walk away, because your life guide was supporting you and literally holding you up! I could not have walked away otherwise, but you were in such a wonderful healing light, and as dark as what 'you' felt, the light radiated all around you. You had the support of your life guide.*

*During a lifetime, many other guides may come and go! They come in during certain learning curbs or phases in your life and then move on. In this way too, these 'lesser' guides are training for the role of 'life guide'. This will also explain to you how sometimes, during my writings to you.*

*You may get a message that someone says, 'Hi!' These are new souls that are being trained in the art of communication, which as I have said many times, is not a simple process but involves their ability to change vibration and frequency levels. Just as you would when tuning a radio station! So believe me, there is much celebration on this side when, where a newly evolved soul is allowed to communicate and as simple as, " Dan says Hi", it has taken Dan much time to be able to do that and he is progressing even further now.*

*We have had a soul trying to come through in this writing today but he has not been able to do so. Never mind, there will be other times. There is no death, only progression! And so, Dear Ones, ends our lesson today.*

*Darling one, love, love and love you, now and more each day in eternity.*

*Yours for all time,*

*Raymond*

***TWENTY FIRST LESSON***

*Darling one,*

*My love, we have been doing so much work together in the astral. Yes we do such work because many souls who have passed over are unenlightened and need a lot of help to realize their new state of consciousness. Most people lead a physical life and that is why it is so important for them to receive spiritual knowledge while still in their earthly existence, for it helps to make the final transition so much easier. As you have learnt my love, that once you have the spiritual knowledge you are able to rise above any physical limitations or boundary.*

*Donald must wait until February to put his new ideas into action for that is when the universal energies will be strong and events will flow more smoothly. Until then, one day at a time!*

*Bert has been extremely busy in the 'arrivals'. You would be amazed at the pace, in which he works, and yet retains a personal touch with each one. Still in spirit he has his pipe. He sends a message of great love and peace to Yvonne. They have evolved together spiritually and peacefully. He knows great changes are taking place in her life and she has all his blessings and all of his love, always.*

*No one will fill his shoes but he says to relax and to enjoy the moment and give 'The Engelsman' a chance. Laughter is the best medicine. He also says he enjoyed the drive in the 'Rav' and to tell Yvonne that it was he who moved the soap in the shower. He is always popping in with surprise visits. He sends all his love and blessings.*

*Today's lesson begins:*

**** The book has come of age and needs to be printed. We have tried through these lessons to give basic understanding of the vital truth of life. God in all his pure energy and light sends the power and truth to you and it is up to each one of you to open yourself up to receiving it. There are no difficult methods to receiving it, just simply open your minds and hearts to this divine flow, realize your oneness with it and have a receptive attitude.*

*Carry with you always the realization of the universal love and protection around you. Live in it always. To come into 'oneness', you enter realms where you are better able to understand ones self. Coming into harmony with the universal energies brings harmony into the mind, body and soul.*

*You therefore also make it possible for spiritual energy to reach you, so that higher laws and truths can be revealed to you, and in doing so become an enlightened one and a channel. This can be used to enlighten others.*

*God created all men in his likeness. He has chosen few. He did however give every man free will and so the prophets, miracle workers and saviors of the world were all created the same, yet they were the ones who recognized and came into realization of the universal source of energy and power available to all.*

*A simple rule to remember is that like attracts like, the way the energy that you put into the universe is returned to you. The more faith you put into everyday life, the more you will receive.*

*By getting in touch with yourself, by opening your mind to the even flow of the God Force energy surrounding you, will improve your life tremendously.*

*It will attract others to improve their lives too, and that in turn purifies the soul. The health of the body and mind depend on how you relate to yourself. Each morning is a fresh beginning, all yesterdays should remain in the past and how you live your today will determine how you live your tomorrows, it's entirely in your own hands. Open you hearts and give out Universal Love always. Blessed be this lesson.*

*Love, love and love you for all eternity.*

*Raymond*

**The End**

## ***About the author:***

*Pamela still continues to live at the South Coast, where she runs RAYBERT LODGE. She continues to help and heal the bereaved and the lost souls of this world who need spiritual guidance and support.*

*Ray continues to send messages through and they are currently working together on a second book.*


*The Author may be contacted at:*

***P.O.Box 21570***
***Umtentweni***
***4235***

*Telephone:*
*+27**(0)39 681 2583***

*or e-mail at:*
**raybert@mweb.co.za**